Therapeutic Adventures

64 activities for therapy outdoors

Roger & Christine Day

Brook Creative Therapy

Copyright © Roger & Christine Day 2008

First published in 2008 by Therapy in Romania
Revised 2011 by Brook Creative Therapy

All rights reserved. No part of this publication may be reproduced or transmitted in any form or by any means, electronic or mechanical, including photocopy, recording or any information storage and retrieval system, without permission in writing from the publisher. Pages may be photocopied for therapeutic, supervisory and training use only provided the copyright line is retained.

Published by:

Brook Creative Therapy, Brook Cottage, 16 Burnside, Rugby, Warwickshire CV22 6AX, UK

Details of how to order further copies can be obtained by emailing brookcreativetherapy@gmail.com

About the authors

Roger Day
Certified Transactional Analyst, Psychotherapist and Play Therapy specialist
For many years Roger has been a trainer and supervisor specialising in children and families. Now retired, he lives in Rugby, Warwickshire.

Christine Day
European Adult Teaching Certificate, Nursery Nurse Examination Board (NNEB), Diploma in Counselling, Certificate in Counselling Skills
Christine is a qualified nursery nurse. In addition to successfully raising four children, over the years she has added play and creativity specialisms to her nursery skills. Christine lives with Roger in Rugby, Warwickshire.

Books by Roger & Christine Day:

Matryoshkas in Therapy: Creative ways to use Russian dolls with clients
Creative Anger Expression
Creative Therapy in the Sand: Using sandtray with clients
Body Awareness: 64 bodywork activities for therapy (2008/2011)
Therapeutic Adventure: 64 activities for therapy outdoors (2008/2011)
Stories that Heal: 64 creative visualisations for use in therapy (2011)

Brook Creative Therapy, Brook Cottage, 16 Burnside, Rugby CV22 6AX, UK

Little Billy's mother was always telling him exactly what he was allowed to do and what he was not allowed to do. All the things he was allowed to do were so boring. All the things he was not allowed to do were exciting.

One of the things he was NEVER NEVER allowed to do, the most exciting of them all, was to go through the garden gate all by himself and explore the world beyond.
– Roald Dahl, **The Minpins**

Acknowledgements

There are several people we would like to thank for helping to make this book possible.

We are grateful to Bob Davis for introducing us to the 'Oak tree's special gift' creative visualisation.

David Dobedoe has been a regular source of encouragement and inspiration in seeing therapeutic adventure become a reality.

Geoff Marshall gave us some ideas and suggestions from his interest in the outdoors, including his extensive knowledge of orienteering and map reading.

Young people Bethan and Siän tested out some of our ideas in the high, icy forests near Padiş, Romania.

We are grateful to Rev Lynda Rowinson, a real-life Vicar of Dibley, for her wealth of creative ideas, and especially for her advice in developing the labyrinth as a useful tool for therapeutic adventure and play therapy.

Roger remembers with fondness Ron Banyard and Lou Stevens, whose love of the outdoors had a profound influence on him during his formative years.

Finally, we want to appreciate the many individuals and groups who have travelled with us on the path to adventure in the great outdoors. We have learned so much from you and from nature itself.

Contents

Introduction

What you will need

Trust
    Rope trail in pairs
    Night walk
    Crowd surfing in nature
    Follow a trail
    Blind walk
    Rope obstacle course
    Flying like Superman
    Pick-me-up

Nature
    Group imagination
    Did you hear something?
    Wow, look at that!
    Make friends with a tree
    Found treasure
    Using your senses
    Nature walk
    Hands and knees

Working together
    Noah's ark
    Shout and point
    Group flying
    Parachute games
    Knotty problem
    Removals
    Broomstick obstacles
    Simple abseil

Survival
- Make a fire
- Water in the wild
- Build a shelter
- Finding your way
- Self-care
- Food from the wild
- Get the message
- Cooking food outside

Confidence
- Exploring in the dark
- Swaying branch
- Scream away
- Stepping across
- Tricky situation
- Confidence booster
- Finding your way up
- Reach for the sky

Risk-taking
- Crossing the water
- Rock clambering
- Run in the dark
- Climb in the treetops
- Mud, glorious mud
- Swing across
- Tightrope walking
- Mexican wave

Achievements
- Aiming straight
- Grasshoppers
- Landmines
- Emergency!
- Hand and feet sculptures
- Mud climb
- Sneakers
- 'My achievements'

Relaxation and enjoyment
    Oak tree's special gift
    My special house
    On your own in nature
    The labyrinth journey
    'I live in the leaves'
    Tree impressions
    Leafy lines and patterns
    Pictures from nature

Sources and references

Appendix 1: Being OK, Keeping OK, by Roger Day

Introduction

At some time in our lives most of us have walked in the mountains, explored a forest or jumped on stepping-stones across a clear, babbling brook. Some of us have abseiled off a cliff, explored a cave or climbed high obstacles and swum through mud on an assault course. Challenges and experiences in nature can be refreshing, exhilarating and awe-inspiring. They can also be frightening, exhausting and frustrating.

Whatever our reactions to such experiences, the memories stay in our minds for years to come. Many of us have a greater feeling of well-being and are more aware of ourselves as a result of experiences in nature.

Now imagine merging such challenges and experiences in nature with therapy led by a trained and experienced therapist and you have what we call 'therapeutic adventure'.

There are many therapeutic models suitable for working outdoors using therapy. We have based these activities on nonverbal play therapy. The activities are designed for use with adults, teenagers and children. All of them work well with groups. Many of the activities can be adapted for work with just one client, assuming that the therapist takes part in the therapeutic activity.

Therapists might ask the question: 'What is the added benefit of doing therapy in nature over working with clients in the comfort of the therapy room?'

Michael Gass and Lee Gillis believe that, when done correctly, information from therapeutic adventure can provide a rich assessment of client behaviour. They write: 'Some of the advantages of adventure experiences include: (a) the combination of ambiguity and stress that coexist in adventure experiences; (b) the increased level of validity in client responses to assessment procedures (eg clients must "walk their talk"); and (c) the ability of therapists to receive appropriate information as well as simultaneously analyse psychological processes and behavioural content' (Gass & Gillis, 1995, page 36).

Our own experience is that therapeutic adventure can result in dramatic and long-lasting emotional changes that may happen much quicker than within the therapy room alone. But, of course, the therapist needs to think in a different way when starting to use therapeutic adventure. There are issues of confidentiality and safety to consider, and it is important to assess clients' needs and make adjustments in the programme in order to meet those needs.

One of the issues in therapeutic adventure that is different from therapy indoors is that of confidentiality. Nick Ray is an outdoor activity instructor and a therapist specialising in Transactional Analysis. When working in the therapy room he makes a confidentiality contract with his (mainly) adult clients. But, he continues, 'when working in the outdoors we can be seen by the general public and so we contract to continue the work even though there may be people present, sometimes within earshot. We decide what we will do at these points when it is no longer private. But having said that, a lot of the time I do endeavour to work where I can create a safe space, but I cannot always guarantee that we will not be interrupted' (Ray, 2005, page 16).

Safety – physical and psychological – is another vital factor to consider. Kaye Richards and Jenny Peel write: 'Even though the outdoors can provide a rich milieu for therapeutic work, it also makes the client more vulnerable than they might be in a more controlled indoor setting. The outdoors has extended psychological and physical risks, eg keeping a group physically safe climbing a mountain. Therefore, working as a therapist in the outdoors expands the role of the therapist to one who may have to manage physical as well as psychological safety' (Richards & Peel, 2005, page 7).

The exercises contained in this book are intended as a basic introduction to therapeutic adventure. They do not need specialist equipment or qualified instructors. However, safety of the participants is such an important issue that we strongly recommend any therapist wanting to use them to become competent in at least some aspects of safety. This might involve going on a first-aid course, doing some training in outdoor leadership or going to the gym regularly and getting fit enough himself/herself to work with clients outdoors.

If you are intending to work with clients in a setting unfamiliar to you, it is essential that you visit the area in advance, do the activities yourself and get to know the area and its potential hazards. You might also consider working in partnership with someone (not necessarily a therapist) more experienced in the outdoors than you. You could then focus on the therapeutic aspects while the other person leads the walk and arranges the areas of forest to work in, etc. If you do this, it is essential that you establish a clear contract of confidentiality with him/her when you are working together with the clients.

Another aspect of safety to consider is insurance. Are you insured to work therapeutically in this setting? If not, what additional insurance do you need? Be aware that insurance companies providing cover for groups have exclusion clauses for hazardous activities that can include mountaineering. Be careful how you explain the activities to them. 'Walking with clients in the mountains' may, in their view, be acceptable and very different from the unacceptable 'mountaineering', which involves climbing gear. If you are taking clients away for a weekend or a week, they would need their own holiday insurance, which may cover some of these insurance needs.

In the case of young people, you will need parents/carers' written permission for many of the activities in this book. You will also need to ensure that clients of any age are medically fit to take part. A carefully worded letter (checked out by a friendly solicitor) that is signed by the client or by a young person's parent/carer could well prevent possible serious problems if in the unlikely event something were to go wrong.

As a therapist working with clients outdoors, it is important that you have ways of monitoring the effectiveness of the therapy. In the case of young people, one way is through a clinical governance measure such as the Strengths and Difficulties Questionnaire (Goodman, 1999). This uses tick-box forms to measure aspects of the young person's emotional and behavioural issues before and after therapy. An additional form of monitoring is to use a specialist outdoor therapy assessment tool. Therapeutic adventure can be assessed using two tools: the GRABBS and the CHANGES models, outlined as follows:

GRABBS (Schoel, Prouty & Radcliffe, 1988) stands for:
Goals What are the goals of the outdoor experience for the group, the individual client and the therapist?

Readiness How ready are the clients for the outdoor activities the therapist is offering?

Affect What is the level of affect (feeling) among the clients?

Behaviour How have the clients behaved so far towards each other, the therapist and the outdoor experience itself?

Body Are the clients treating each other's bodies with respect?

Stage What stage is the group at (Forming? Norming? Performing? Mourning? – see Tuckman, 1965)?

The GRABBS model can be used in conjunction with the CHANGES assessment model (Gass & Gillis, 1995):

Context Where is the therapist working and what are the goals? What previous experiences can inform the therapist? What competencies does he/she possess, and what extra research/training is needed to ensure success in therapeutic adventure?

Hypothesising What information about working with clients in the therapist's past experience can be used as a hypothesis for understanding clients' behaviour? What formal sources (such as assessment tools) and informal sources (such as intuitive assessment of group engagement in activities) can inform this hypothesis?

Action that is Novel In what ways do the clients' responses to a novel therapeutic adventure experience confirm the therapist's initial hypotheses? How might the therapist adapt, revise or reject his/her thoughts in the light of observable response to the activities? What other interventions might be effective, based on seeing the real issues of the client, not just those seen at the social level?

Generating information, stories and ideas What verbal stories or behavioural information is the therapist getting that can generate therapeutic objectives and procedures? What nonverbal ideas is he/she obtaining in the areas of clients' values and beliefs? How are the clients functioning within the outdoor group in terms of closeness, intimacy, roles and power? What therapeutic needs do the clients have, and how can these be met?

Evaluation What tentative decisions has the therapist come to in terms of: symptoms and diagnosis; clients' motivation, strengths and needs; and possible interventions? Which hypotheses are confirmed and which rejected by the clients' behaviour?

Solutions What potential client solutions can be identified and constructed as a result of the evaluation process? What would be effective in helping to solve the clients' therapeutic issues?

For therapists new to working outdoors, or who would like further background information, read Roger Day's article 'Being OK, Keeping OK' in Appendix 1.

The book *Therapeutic Adventure* contains 64 activities divided into eight sections. The activities can be photocopied and laminated for use. These activities can be used for any therapeutic individual or group work. They can be used in a directive or nondirective way.

In nondirective individual therapy the client might choose a card at random and, with the therapist's help, take part in the activity. In directive group or individual therapy the therapist selects cards in advance and encourages the individual or whole group to take part. Pages from the different sections could be used or the emphasis could be on one or two categories.

Please note that not all the activities are suitable for every client. The therapist knows his/her clients and can select those most suitable or remove those that he/she considers unsuitable or unhelpful for a particular client.

Roger & Christine Day

What you will need

The activities included in this book need the minimum of equipment and materials. The following is a summary:

Equipment for activities

Each activity includes a list of equipment/materials needed. The following list is not comprehensive but will give you a guide about the sort of things needed:

Strong rope – at least 10 metres in length, although the activities will still work if you use several ropes tied together
Blindfolds or scarves
Matches
Magnifying glass
Compass
Map of the local area
Torch
Paper, coloured card and boards (hardcover books could be used instead of boards)
Glue
Pencils, thick crayons, felt-tip pens

Outdoor equipment for leaders

First-aid kit
Suntan cream
Insect repellent
Local map
Compass
Whistle
Waterproof matches
Thermal blanket and survival bag (available from camping stores)
Walkie-talkies or GPS indicator – mobile phones often do not work in the mountains
Toilet paper

Antiseptic no-water hand wash

Items needed for each client

Back pack
Drinks
High energy food (Mars bars or similar)
Stout shoes or trainers
Waterproof coat
Extra sweater
Spare socks

Warning: Check local weather conditions before setting out on walks, climbing up mountains or going into forests. Find out about local mountain rescue services. Write down telephone numbers and learn about international rescue signals (see Get the Message in this book).

Prepare for the worst possible conditions, from wet to cold to extreme heat. Exposure is a hazard in the UK, even in summer. Orange survival bags fit over the head and right down the body of a crouching person while waiting for rescue. A tiny thermal blanket can mean the difference between life and death for someone suffering the beginnings of hypothermia.

In hot climates do not travel outside in the middle of the day (between, say, 12.00 and 16.00). In these areas, ensure that everyone (children included) drinks at least two litres of liquid a day. Sometimes even more is necessary. An early indication of dehydration is going for long periods of not needing to urinate. If this happens, people need to drink urgently even if they don't feel like it. If clients start to feel faint, it may be because they have lost too much salt through sweating. Carry salt tablets in case of heat exhaustion. Wash these down with plenty of water. If possible, avoid salt in water, which can lead to vomiting.

Beware of adders, whose bite could kill, and bees, wasps and certain spiders, whose bite can cause a lot of pain. Other hazards in North America include wolves and bears, plus in Romania and other central European countries wild boar.

Trust

Introduction

The dictionary defines 'trust' as the 'assured reliance on the character, ability, strength or truth of someone or something' and involves 'believing in the honesty and reliability of others'.

Trust is fundamental to human existence. Erik Erickson described the basic trust developed by babies in the first months of life as the 'cornerstone of a vital personality' (Erikson, 1968, page 97). Trust involves the person developing a sense of being trustworthy as well as having trust in others. Erikson saw discovering basic trust as the first task of the ego, and that it is never complete. He believed that the balance of trust with mistrust depended largely on the quality of the maternal (or other) relationship. Later, because of situations of vulnerability, even those clients who have developed a sense of trust may need to revisit this area in order to learn trust again.

This trust must be balanced with healthy paranoia or it can lead to gullibility. In the case of adopted and fostered children with attachment issues, for instance, such children sometimes display an over-familiarity with all adults. This lack of mistrust could lead to serious child protection issues.

Wilson and Ryan (1992/2005) point out that 'an essential component of therapy for children is having trust in their therapists. Similarly to carers, therapists' sensitivity to what each child needs, as well as therapists' firm sense of their own trustworthiness as an adult, needs to be combined with therapists' belief in children's ability to develop in an emotionally health way' (page 69).

Outdoor activities involving a considerable level of trust in other people can help with the process. James Neill, a psychologist specialising in outdoor education, writes: 'Trust-building activities can break down barriers and build deep feelings of trust and reliance between individuals and within small groups' (Neill, 2007).

He gives a word of caution about introducing such activities too early in a programme. He believes that group members need to have come to accept each other and demonstrated individual responsibility first.

Once the activity has been done, he recommends a time of discussion. 'Processing, reflecting on and communicating about trust experiences can help participants to explore and better understand their feelings and reactions to trust-building activities and their relationships with others involved in the activities' (Neill, 2007).

Rope trail in pairs

Materials needed

A rope.

Instructions

This exercise (illustrated on the front cover) involves working in pairs. One person is blindfolded and the partner is sighted. The sighted person needs to look after the other person. The idea is that they both follow a rope up a steep hill, with the person who can see verbally guiding (but not touching) the other person as best he/she can to reach the top. There is no hurry. It is more important to get there safely and comfortably. At the top, the person removes the blindfold and looks back on what was achieved. Then the blindfolds are swapped around, the rope is moved to a different position and the pairs go up the rope again.

    As the facilitator it is important that you ensure safety as the pairs go up the rope. Make sure they are not too close to each other. Also, someone with a blindfold on will not see a sharp twig at head height that could cause a cut or even a head injury. Climbing on to a wet or moss-covered rock may result in a slip, and a short comment from you could save an injury.

    For people experienced in outdoor activities, make the climb quite difficult – over rocks, even through low branches if possible. This will challenge both partners and hopefully result in even greater fun.

Objectives

This exercise is about trust. The blindfolded person learns to trust his/her partner and follow verbal instructions, even when the way seems unclear. The sighted person learns about being an effective leader, taking responsibility for someone else.

Night walk

Materials needed

Torches for the leaders and, if possible, some of the participants.

Instructions

If clients have never gone on a nature walk in the dark it can be an extremely frightening experience for some of them. Be prepared for some of them to become nervous or even panicky.

Choose a route in advance that is reasonably safe and free from dangers such as deep mud, barbed wire or low tree branches. Set out with torches on, then once you are away from the lights of any buildings, stop and switch off the torches. Encourage the participants to get their night vision. Suggest they observe, listen and overcome any fear they have. This usually takes several minutes.

Once they are ready, begin to walk without torches. After a short distance switch them on again and continue with the walk. Do this frequently, then stop for a longer time, encouraging clients to explore their immediate surroundings in complete darkness. They may want to talk about what the experience is like for them. Be prepared for some surprising admission of fear, often from the toughest-looking participants!

When you have returned, spend some time in the light talking or engaging in games to help people relax. Going straight to bed after an experience in the dark such as this could result in increased fears or nightmares.

Objectives

This exercise enhances observation skills and increases self-care and sensory acuity. Be aware that people who have been traumatised sometimes lose their ability to enjoy certain senses. This is a safe way of helping them recapture those lost senses.

Crowd surfing in nature

Materials needed

None.

Instructions

Crowd Surfing in Nature involves a group of people raising one of its members above their heads in a horizontal position facing upwards, and then carrying the person across a field or through a clearing in the forest.

Choose a spot that is free of obstructions that could trip people over. It is essential that the group has already gelled together because this exercise involves considerable trust. The person who is to be carried lies back into the arms of the team. It is best for the person to fold arms, relax and keep eyes closed. The team then carefully lift the person (the distributed weight makes this fairly easy) and walk across the field with him or her. When they reach the other side of the field, they carefully lower the person to the ground.

Continue the activity until everyone who wants to has had a turn. Some of the clients may want more than one turn.

Objectives

This is an exercise in trust, concentration and group development. It is also plenty of fun. It may be a useful experience for you and the participants if *you* become the person being carried.

Follow a trail

Materials needed

Salt-free and sugar-free popcorn or other biodegradable material that is easy to see. If you are making popcorn, which we recommend, you will need several panfuls. You could consider getting clients to help, or even make it themselves (ensuring that if they are young people they are safe – the temperature at which corn pops is 200-300 degrees Celsius).

Instructions

Follow a Trail has similarities to the old-fashioned paper trail except it uses biodegradable material. Ideally, get the participants into groups of three. One person in each group sets the trail through the forest by scattering popcorn along the route, then hiding at the end. The other two have to find the first person by following the trail. The element of trust is that one of the two people walks backwards and the partner guides him/her by words only. Once the three are united, they swap places and continue until all three have had a turn setting the trail, being the verbal guide and walking backwards.

Make sure the trail is not set too early or the popcorn will all be eaten by birds and small creatures. Also, as the facilitator it is important that you know which direction each of the groups has gone so that if there are any difficulties you can follow their trail and find them.

Objectives

This is an exercise in teamwork and trust. The person laying the trail will need to learn not to make it too difficult for the others. The one walking backwards will need to trust his/her partner, while the partner will need to be aware of forest hazards such as roots and brambles and take care of the one walking backwards as much as possible.

Blind walk

Materials needed

A blindfold for each participant.

Instructions

This exercise involves one person going on a walk in the wilds (hills, forest, etc) with the rest of the group following. The difference here is that everyone except the person in front is blindfolded for the whole walk.

Before starting the walk get the clients to decide how those who are blindfolded will know where to go. They could follow verbal signals, hold hands or hold waists. Give the participants the choice.

You might take the lead, or you might get a client to take the lead. Bear in mind that if one participant leads, many of the others will want a turn, too.

A variation could be one person leading while you join the rest of the participants wearing a blindfold. Bear in mind that, unless you have another assistant with you, there is a slight risk if you as well as most of the clients are blindfolded.

Objectives

The objective of this exercise is to facilitate teamwork and trust. Giving the participants a choice in how communication is achieved encourages taking initiative and building confidence.

Rope obstacle course

Materials needed

A length of rope.

Instructions

The object of this exercise is for a group of people to go through an obstacle course in the forest or a rocky area blindfolded, guided by a rope. If you have enough participants, divide them into two teams. One teams sets up the obstacle course with natural objects and the other team goes through it, with instructions from the first team. Then they swap around and set up a new course.

As the facilitator, you can encourage the team setting up the course to involve the whole team in discussing how they will set it up and instruct the other team. Everyone needs to be involved in the discussion and planning. If you notice that one or two of the team members are being left out or one is telling everyone else what to do, it is important to point this out and encourage the involvement of each person.

Objectives

This exercise promotes trust, planning, teamwork and creativity in finding effective solutions. By involving everyone, you are ensuring that clients' self-esteem and confidence are built up.

Flying like Superman

Materials needed

None.

Instructions

Almost all young people – and adults – would like to fly like Superman. This activity enables them to experience something as near to that as possible.

You will need a group of at least 11 clients who are functioning well together – one to be Superman and a minimum of 10 to act as catchers. The idea is that Superman leaps up and off a rock, log or slight hill rise and is caught by the others as he/she falls. Then another Superman has a turn, and so on until everyone in the group who wants to has flown.

Both the catchers and Superman need careful instruction. The catchers need to stand close together in two lines facing each other, arms stretched out and overlapping to form a kind of net. They need to bend their arms and keep their fingers beside the elbows of the opposite person. However, it is essential that no one holds on to arms or hands because this could result in banged heads.

Superman needs to dive upwards into the sky, arms high and straight, then fall into their arms. It is important to keep the body stiff and straight, with no bending of knees. If this happens it can put too much weight and pressure on a few of the catchers.

You or another helper needs to watch carefully, preferably from where Superman jumps, to ensure that the line of catchers is ready and in position. Otherwise the leap could be dangerous.

A more advanced variation is to do the leap blindfolded. Make sure that participants have practiced well before attempting this.

Warning: If at any point a participant decides to fool around, he or she needs to be withdrawn from this particular activity immediately because safety is of the utmost importance.

Objectives

This is an activity that involves considerable trust. People whose trust has been tested in the past, through abuse or in other areas, are likely to find it extremely difficult. It may take time and patience for clients to take the leap. Once they do, though, they are likely to have a wonderful and exhilarating experience.

Pick-me-up

Materials needed

One or two small natural objects such as pinecones.

Instructions

Pick-me-up is a group activity in which a blindfolded person crosses a clearing in the forest (or an open field) and picks up a pinecone, or something similar, returning with it to the starting point.

The rest of the team help in different ways. One person acts as the Voice. He/she stands back to back with the blindfolded person and isn't allowed to look at the clearing/field. The rest of the team act as Instructors. They stand in front of the Voice where he/she can see them without seeing the clearing. They are not allowed to speak. Rather, they use hand and body gestures that the Voice then explains to the blindfolded person.

The object of the activity is for the blindfolded person to move across the clearing, pick up the object and return to the starting point, putting it into the Voice's hands. Then the next person takes turn being blindfolded.

If you are working with a large group, split them into teams of about five or six. You might consider having a competition between the two (or more) teams, seeing which one can return the pinecone fastest.

A variation of this is to place the pinecones in opposite corners of the clearing so that the two blindfolded people have to cross each other's path in order to get the object.

Objectives

The objective of Pick-me-up is trust in other people's communication and sense of direction. In order for it to succeed, every team member needs to be involved. People who have struggled with trust issues in their life may at first find this difficult. For instance, some people who have been abused may be terrified of putting such trust in other people. But the sense of achievement when they bring the object back could be a transforming experience for them. Pick-me-up is a reasonably safe activity that most people will enjoy.

Nature

Introduction

> I stroll along serenely,
> with my eyes,
> my shoes,
> my rage,
> forgetting everything.
> *Pablo Neruda*

The damaged teenage girl stood getting her breath back at the top of the mountain. It was her first visit to the wilds and she was hating every minute of the experience.

'Look at that,' said the instructor, pointing out the beautiful vista across mountains, valleys and woodlands. 'Isn't it amazing?'

'Nah, it's boring,' she replied flatly. 'It's all just green.'

'Look again,' he said. 'There's loads of different greens. Can you see all the things that are different shades of green?'

'Yeah, I guess so. Hey, look at that. There's a bit of brown right in the middle of that patch of light green and dark green!'

For this girl, like so many other people, young and old, discovering nature can be the beginning of a major emotional healing. Being alone or with a few others in the wilds can be a tonic to life's pressures and a release of joy and breaking free from the past.

Dyer writes: 'People instinctively turn to outdoor and nature-loving activities as a way of relaxing and enhancing their well-being. Nature can aid in facilitating self-awareness and promoting healing. For many the outdoors is a source of inspiration, solace, guidance and regeneration' (Dyer, 2002).

Exposure to nature can reduce the symptoms of hyperactivity (ADHD). This is the remarkable conclusion of a study of 400 children aged 5 to 18 by the University of Illinois at Urbana-Champaign. 'In the study, kids who participated in "green outdoor activities" had significantly reduced symptoms, regardless of geography, urban or rural environment, diagnosis, age, sex or income group' (*USA Weekend,* 2005).

For many of us, the natural world has been a haven to escape from the crazy world around us. 'Nature can become a place of refuge for difficult times. When life stresses start closing in, one can escape to the wilderness physically or mentally. Being in nature helps to clear one's head of life's demands and disruptive thoughts. This clarity of thought may lead to finding answers to life's questions and discovering insights to life's problems' (Dyer, 2002).

Group imagination

Materials needed

None.

Instructions

Invite the clients to find a comfortable place in nature to lie down. It could be a clearing in the forest or a grassy field. Get them to close their eyes and concentrate on their breathing. Then they need to let their imaginations roam.

Explain that when an image comes to someone's mind, they speak it out and describe it. *Note: You might need some rules about politeness when working with young people. Boys of a particular age are likely to think only of rude things!*

The rest of the group listen and add images as they come to their minds. When the ideas about that image are exhausted, they stop. Someone else then talks about an image they can see.

Assure people not to worry about long silences. They are part of the process of group imagination.

The group imagination can continue as long as ideas keep flowing. You may be surprised how long even young people can keep their imaginations flowing.

Objectives

This exercise helps with creativity, team building, imagination and relaxation. Be aware that it may prove difficult for hyperactive clients, because of keeping still, and those on the autistic spectrum, because of their literal thinking. Apart from that, it can be a fun and enlightening way for clients to express themselves safely in a natural setting.

Did you hear something?

Materials needed

None.

Instructions

This is an exercise in focusing on sounds in nature and then discussing them.

Get the client/s to find a comfortable place in nature to sit or preferably lie down. Make sure they are well apart from each other. Then invite them to close their eyes. They need to be in complete silence. Invite them to listen to all the sounds they can hear. A way to help them focus is first for them to become aware of their own breathing and heartbeat – if they can hear them. Then they can start becoming aware of the sounds around us.

You may give them clues. You may want to use phrases such as: 'Be aware of any sound of wind or movement in the trees or grass. Are there any bird sounds you can hear? What other sounds can you hear? If you notice a sound, focus on it. Tune your ears until you hear it clearly.'

Don't be in a hurry with this exercise. Part of the aim is relaxation and enjoyment. After you finish, give them a couple of minutes, then invite them to open their eyes and look at you or the other people around them. This helps them to anchor and return to the present.

Finally, invite them as an individual/group to list all the sounds they heard. What ones could they identify and what ones remained a mystery? What sounds did they like and what did they dislike?

Objectives

This exercise helps to heighten clients' sensory awareness and increase concentration skills. It also enables them to get encouragement (in the form of positive strokes) for what they have noticed.

Wow, look at that!

Materials needed

None.

Instructions

Help the client/s to find a comfortable place to sit down. A good place would be at the top of a mountain or hill where the view is very clear and attractive. Then encourage them to allow their eyes to focus on what they can see. Explain that this exercise is about concentrating on particular natural objects, near or in the distance.

Give them a couple of minutes to look, then ask if the person or group member is ready to point something out to you or the rest of the group. You or the group then looks at what the person is focusing on. It may take a minute or two before everyone is looking at the right object.

Then the you and the client or the group together describe the object in terms of colour, texture, distance from them and relationship to other objects. If they get stuck, they may need some prompting from you as the facilitator. Someone might say that a plant is green. Ask questions such as: 'What sort of green? Light or dark, plain or patterned?' Keep going until they are flowing in their words once again.

Once the focusing on and description of an object is exhausted, get someone else to point out his or her object. If possible, ensure that every group member, even the quietest one, has a turn at the focusing.

Objectives

This is an exercise in concentration, group development, sensory awareness and encouragement of each other. Clients who have very little confidence will be delighted when you or everyone in the group starts talking about 'their' object. Clients whose senses have been dulled through trauma or abuse may find this fairly harmless activity both fun and helpful in reawakening their senses.

Make friends with a tree

Materials needed

Blindfolds.

Instructions

Choose a pleasant, forested area. Get the clients to form pairs, one wearing a blindfold and the other acting as the guide. Make sure that the blindfolded people are well cared for. This includes ensuring that blindfolded people are always holding a hand or touching a tree.

The blindfolded person is the one who makes friends with his (or her) tree. The other person leads him through the trees and places his hands on a special tree. The blindfolded person explores the tree with his hands, getting to know what it is like. It might help to talk about the size of the tree, its shape and angle of growth, the texture of the bark and any smells he can detect. He is then led back to the starting point, takes off his blindfold and tries to locate his tree. After everyone has finished, the pairs swap roles. Sometimes clients will want to have more than one go at being blindfolded.

After everyone has had time to make friends with at least one tree, get the whole group to come back together and discuss what the experience was like. What did people notice about textures and smells and how easy (or difficult) was it to identify the tree?

Objectives

Therapeutic objectives for Make Friends with a Tree include trust building, focusing and sensory attunement. It provides close contact with nature and includes elements of trust and confidence building.

Found treasure

Materials needed

None.

Instructions

This is an ideal activity for including as part of a nature walk. Explain to the clients before you start: 'While we are walking today, look for something that is a treasure to you, something that is very special. When you are happy with what you've found, bring it back to talk about when we have finished.'

Many people appreciate something tangible to help them remember a happy memory from the trip. Some people, particularly adults, may want to bring back a memory, a sight or a new friendship – intangibles that mean something special to them.

When the walk is finished ask the clients to talk about what they have found. Avoid putting your own interpretation on what they show you (or talk about). It is important to listen to their words and what the found treasure means to them.

Objectives

This exercise enables clients to enhance their awareness and appreciation of something new. It helps them to look from a different, nonmaterialistic perspective, really appreciating things that money can't buy. For example, they can't take a waterfall home but they can take home the memory. When others focus uncritically on what they have found it can build their confidence and self-esteem. The type of treasure found by the clients can be used by the therapist as part of her/his assessment of the client's emotional needs.

Using your senses

Materials needed

None.

Instructions

Prepare in advance pieces of paper with five columns on them. Label the columns as the five senses – touch, taste, smell, sight, sound. If you are working with very young children you may need to use small pictures rather than words to indicate the different senses. Give one Five Senses paper to each person and get them to explore nature with their own senses, writing down or drawing as many examples as they can find of how they might receive comfort, pleasure and enjoyment through those senses in nature.

Be careful with the sense of taste because of possible poisonous berries or plants. You might need to introduce a safety element. For instance, instead of actually tasting items, they might see something that reminds them of a good taste. For example, a red berry might remind them of a fruit they like or a toadstool could remind them of the taste of freshly fried mushrooms.

Once they have something in all five columns, they can find a partner and share with him or her what they have discovered. For young children, they might get into small groups to share their discoveries with an adult present.

Back in the main group ask the participants questions such as: 'Were you surprised by what you listed?' 'Were some of the senses used less than others?' This may help to promote discussion about the senses.

Offer the clients (and maybe yourself) a challenge. Suggest they see if they can consciously experience pleasure from each sense every day.

Objectives

People who are traumatised, anxious or depressed tend to lose some of their sensory awareness. It is a fact, for instance, that depressed people and those who have been abused tend to have the shortest lists of senses in this exercise. After therapy they develop longer lists. Helping clients to develop sensory acuity may well help them to deal with their problems even more effectively.

Nature walk

Materials needed

It is recommended that each client has a backpack containing a drink in a plastic bottle, an energy bar (Mars bar or similar), a spare pair of socks in case of getting wet and a raincoat. If you are going for the day, make sure they have some lunch as well. The facilitator and helper/s need first aid kit, map, compass, at least two walkie-talkies and possibly a mobile phone, if it works in the area you are walking. Also have enough small boxes (such as matchboxes) so that each client has at least one.

Instructions

Walking with clients in nature can be fun and exhilarating both for the clients and the facilitator/s. Without sufficient preparation, however, it can become gruelling, exhausting and discouraging. It is best if at least two facilitators are involved, one leading the walk and the other staying at the back to ensure that the slowest participants keep moving. Each facilitator needs a walkie-talkie or mobile phone in case of emergencies or if some of the party get left behind.

Choose a route with plenty of variety. You might consider an area including forest, mountains, a river or stream and grassy areas. *It is strongly advised that you walk the route before taking clients on it.*

Give each client a matchbox or similar at the beginning of the walk, inviting them to collect interesting things as they go along. A few rules are important. One is about leaving behind any living things. We once took young people from an inner city area on a nature walk. One boy collected colourful snails, filling his pockets with them. When he got back he was told to throw them away. He did – into a bin in the boys' bedroom. Later there were snails crawling all over the room, in beds and over luggage!

Another important rule is about not picking wild flowers. In many countries, it is illegal to do so. It makes sense anyway to leave flowers where they are for others to enjoy rather than allowing them to wilt and die within a couple of hours.

As you walk, stop, let all the participants catch up and point out birds, mammals, insects and plants. Lift up stones and rocks and look for creepy-crawlies, frogs, toads and lizards. Encourage the participants to call out when they see something new, then get everyone else to gather around while the person shows everyone the item.

Use the nature walk to discuss ways of looking after nature and respecting it. How can they help to ensure that there is a beautiful world for the next generation?

On a practical note, make sure the participants have enough to drink on the journey, especially in hot weather. If they get wet feet, suggest they change their socks. There is nothing more discouraging than walking with wet feet.

Once the walk is finished, get the clients to open their matchboxes in turn and show what they have collected. Ensure that everyone takes an interest in each person's contribution, however small.

Objectives

A nature walk helps clients to feel safe in nature and aware of their surroundings. It is an enjoyable experience and can build their confidence in finding and talking about objects. Assisting each other to cross streams and get through muddy patches can be good for teambuilding.

Hands and knees

Materials needed

Magnifying glasses, bug boxes and possibly nets and dishes for pond dipping. Books on insects, spiders and mites, pond life. Possibly tent pegs and string.

Instructions

This is an activity in which clients can observe nature at very close quarters. It is a great activity for adults and for children of all ages. Children as young as three or four often find it just as fascinating as sophisticated adults.

Choose an area of the forest preferably clear of ants that bite. (Remember, however, that some clients find ants so interesting that they might be ready to put up with a few bites!) Both you and the clients then get down very low and start looking at the insects and other small creatures crawling through the leaves. It is probably less tiring to get on hands and knees than to bend low for a long time. Then invite the participants to use magnifying glasses and bug boxes to study the creatures they find. Listen for clients finding something different and get the rest of the group to look at it. Together try to identify the creatures you find, using any books you have with you.

Hands and Knees is a good exercise in other locations, too. Get everyone to crouch down low and lift a rock, observing the little creatures as they run for another hiding place. Crouch around a pile of animal dung and see the variety of beetles and other creatures that feed there. Get down close to watch ants carrying large pieces of food along a particular narrow route. Dip nets into ponds, put everything (mud and all) into dishes of clear water and study the many tiny creatures swimming around.

As an alternative to working in the large group, get each person to find a partner and work in pairs to encourage cooperation. At the end of a set time each pair tells the rest of the group about what they have found.

For adults and enthusiastic older children, consider using tent pegs and string to make a square of a particular size and see how many different types of creature they can find in that area. Then choose another location and observe the creatures in an area of the same size.

Objectives

This exercise can help clients to feel safe and not threatened by the creepy-crawlies they find. It encourages cooperation and communication skills when people report to the rest of the group. Focusing on tiny creatures in such an intense way can help the group process. Giving permission for people of any age to get muddy knees can be therapeutic in itself!

Working together

Introduction

Working in a group enables clients to understand the way they relate to others. It provides the space to resolve problems by testing past history with current reality. The group leader facilitates this process through empathy, clear boundaries and holding the group together.

A group takes on a life independent of its members. 'Group dynamics are evident in practically any situation in which individuals interact on a meaningful basis: When they have awareness of each other's presence, an insight into others' motivation and an expectation of what the outcome of their interaction with others might be . . . That unity of purpose introduces dynamic processes that affect decision making roles, the collective motivation of the group, the methods of communication and other features that cannot exist at an individual level. Like the brushes and pails of the sorcerer's apprentice, the group takes on a life of its own' (Cashmore, 2002, pages 127-8).

Tuckman (1965) wrote about the stages a group usually goes through: Forming, Storming, Norming, Performing. Berne (1963/1973) also developed four stages for a group (provisional, adapted, operative, adjusted), which he called imagoes (how a group member imagines the rest of the group).

In both cases group endings were missed out and added by others later. Endings are important in groups. Leben (1993-9) talks about the importance of therapeutic terminations with children's groups, suggesting that the group holds a special ceremony for the leaving group member. The same kind of ending would be useful with adult groups.

Napper & Newton (2000) put Berne's imagoes and Tuckman's stages together to produce what we summarise as:

Imagine – forming

There's me, the leader and all these others.

Meet – storming

Conflict and rebellion.

Angling – norming

Cohesion of the group, jostling to find a place.

Get on – performing

Moving to calling it 'my group'. Recognising others. Giving and getting strokes.

Clarified – mourning

Space for grief, consideration of 'What next?'

Some group activities involve competition. As part of the maturing process, most people develop team-playing skills. Playing in a team involves 'accepting and playing according to team norms, performing a role in a division of labour and assisting others in a way that will facilitate the achievement of team goals' (Cashmore, 2002, page 256).

Noah's ark

Materials needed

Blindfolds for all the participants.

Instructions

This exercise is ideally done with larger groups (say, over 10 people). If you are working with a small group, adapt the instructions accordingly.

The object is to form pairs (or small groups) of animals of the same kind. The participants are blindfolded and in a field or forest clearing. No words are allowed. The only way they can communicate to find each other is by using animal noises.

Each person will need to wear a blindfold. They might help each other to put on the blindfolds, with you assisting where necessary. When they are all ready, go around and whisper to each person the name of an animal. Ensure that there are two and preferably three animals of the same kind. Suggestions could be monkey, elephant, crocodile, bee, tiger and mouse. Explain to the participants that their task is to find all the other animals of the same kind and get together in a small group. Emphasise that they are only to use the animal noises.

The exercise usually results in loud chaos, then settles down to order and unity as people start finding each other. The group leader's task is to ensure safety, especially on uneven ground.

Objectives

This activity is an ideal one for releasing energy. It helps with team building and concentrative skills. Above all, it is plenty of chaotic fun.

Shout and point

Materials needed

None.

Instructions

This is a great game for outside, especially in areas completely away from human habitation. If you do it anywhere near other people, make sure they know that there will be a lot of noise. Because of its intensity and the need for eye contact, it is probably not suitable for participants of any age who are on the autistic spectrum.

Get the clients to form a circle so that they can see everyone else in the circle. Explain that there are two simple instructions that they are asked to follow: 'Heads down' and 'Heads up'. When 'Heads up' is called everyone looks straight into the eyes of someone else in the group. If the other person is looking elsewhere, nothing happens. If two people are looking directly at each other, they are both to point at each other in a very exaggerated way and shout or scream loudly. They are then out of the game. They leave the circle and stay together outside it to watch the rest of the game. When they have left, the others close the circle and the game continues until everyone is out, even the last two.

Once they get used to the action, participants will probably want to take part in the game several times.

Afterwards, you might want to consider asking questions such as: 'What made this fun?' (The answer is probably the stress involved.) 'What are the stresses involved?' ('Will my scream sound silly?' or possibly: 'Will I embarrass myself?') 'When did the stress lessen or increase?' ('When I felt confident.')

Objectives

This activity promotes fun, enjoyment, overcoming embarrassment and a wonderful release of aggression. It can build confidence and help a group to gel with each other in a very funny way.

Group flying

Materials needed

None

Instructions

Most of us as children loved the idea of spreading our arms and flying. In this activity participants of all ages can do the next best thing.

This activity is best done with a group of about six to eight people. The idea is that the group carries one of its members around an area of the forest or a field as if he or she were flying. The person is carried face down, with arms spread out like wings.

The important thing is to start slowly and with extreme care. As the facilitator, it is your role to make sure that each group member is safe when flying. Also, be aware about where the person is being touched so that no one is upset. A good way is to link arms so that the person rests on arms rather than hands. The group gradually increases the speed until the person is flying around quite rapidly.

Make sure that everyone in the group has a turn at flying – if they want to.

Objectives

This is a fun activity based on trust, cooperation and listening to instructions. It can only be successful when the whole group is working together effectively.

Parachute games

Materials needed

Play parachute. Select a size suitable for the group you are working with.

Instructions

Chose an area of the forest or a flat, grassy area that is free of sharp stones and branches that could tear the parachute or injure the participants. Pull the parachute out of the bag and pass part of the edge to one person. Then each participant in turn takes another part of the edge. This is easiest done if the parachute has handles, though holding a handle is not essential.

Once everyone is holding the edge, including you, get the participants to move around the edge until they are evenly spaced, holding with their knuckles on top. Keep the parachute tight and at waist level. Then, together, raise the parachute and allow it to fall naturally. This causes it to billow up. This is best done using a steady count.

Mushroom

Raise and lower the parachute and then, as it is rising, the participants all take one step towards the centre. With practice this creates a mushroom shape. As the parachute comes down again, everyone moves back one step.

Story time

Squat around the parachute, holding on. Stand up together and lift arms to fill the parachute with air. Run two steps forward, pull the parachute over your heads and sit down on the edge of the parachute. If you are working with young children, they may prefer to rush into the middle and sit down. The secret story house falls slowly on everyone. While you are all sitting inside, you might tell a story, use a creative visualisation or sing songs.

Special messages

Place a ball in the middle of the parachute. Practice rolling the ball around the parachute carefully so that it is controlled. Once everyone is ready, call one person's name and everyone helps to roll the ball slowly and gently towards that person. Make sure that everyone gets a 'special message' in this way. For adults and older young people, consider writing a special message in advance for each person, folding up the paper and sending it to the person using the parachute.

Roundabout

Take hold of the parachute with left hands, keeping it tight. Everyone then walks in the same direction. Change hands and go around the other way. Try increasing the speed of walking and the speed of direction change. Try hopping, jumping or skipping as you go around.

Washing machine

This activity needs a small child to volunteer. The child sits in the middle on top of the parachute. Everyone else slowly walks around in a circle holding the parachute loosely. As the facilitator, make sure the parachute is kept below the child's chin. When the child is firmly bound by the parachute several times, everyone pulls back together and the child spins around as if he or she were in a washing machine.

Numbers game

Give the participants a number from one to three so that there is more than one person for each number. Lift the parachute up and down and the third time up shout a number. Those people with that number swap places under the parachute before it falls to earth. No running is allowed. They need to aim for gaps, keep their eyes open and avoid bumping into one another. Make sure that the participants who remain around the edge allow the parachute to fall rather than pulling it down hard.

Hand to hand

Get the participants to hold the parachute tight and pass it to their neighbour in a circle from hand to hand. Young children may find this quite difficult. Make sure the larger participants don't pull the parachute too hard, causing friction burns to the little ones.

Mexican wave

One person raises his or her arms, while holding on to the parachute. This action is repeated around the circle one at a time to create a wave similar to the Mexican wave at a football stadium.

Round and round the world

Place a large plastic ball on one side of the parachute. The group then work together to get the ball to go round and round the world (the parachute). This game in particular needs a lot of cooperation and coordination.

Life's a breeze

Choose some participants to lie under the parachute, facing upwards. They may want to close their eyes or keep them open. You could choose people by gender, those who are wearing say blue or those with brown hair. Everyone else raises and lowers the parachute over the people underneath to create a breeze. Make sure that everyone has a turn to lie underneath the parachute.

Shark attack

Everyone sits on the ground with their legs stretched out under the parachute, which is held at chest height. One person crawls around under the canopy and is the 'shark'. The others make waves with the parachute so that the shark is not seen. He/she quietly grabs the legs of anyone around the perimeter. The person grabbed emits a blood-curdling scream and disappears under the parachute. That person, too, then becomes a shark. Stop just before everyone is under the parachute being a shark. (This is quite a scary game that even young children can enjoy.)

When you have finished parachute games, grasp the parachute at the centre, twist it slightly into a rope shape, wind it round your arm and stow it in the bag.

Objectives

Many of these parachute games are intended to promote teambuilding, confidence, cooperation and above all happy and carefree fun. Use a parachute regularly when working with a group of clients to help build team unity and provide a healthy dose of safe competition.

Knotty problem

Materials needed

None.

Instructions

In this activity the participants tie themselves in a knot by joining hands across the circle. The idea is to undo the knot without letting go of hands.

Get people to form a circle, standing shoulder to shoulder, as close to each other as possible. They then each put a hand in the middle of the circle and hold someone's hand. Invite them to shake hands with the other person and say hello. Then they put their other hand in the middle and take someone else's hand. They say hello to this person, too.

Instruct them to keep hold of the hands because they haven't finished yet. Their next task is to untangle themselves so that they are all standing in a circle with hands held. To do this they must keep their hands clasped. They can change the grip they have on another person's hand, but they must not let go.

After about 10 minutes there is usually evidence of some progress. Then the knotty problem will probably sort itself out quite quickly. If there is no progress, allow the group to unclasp and reclasp one pair of hands. The group needs to negotiate which pair of hands is best suited to the task.

As the facilitator, keep at a moderate distance so as not to give people the impression that they are being observed too closely. Notice those who do the talking, those who are the leaders and those who become passive. Encourage those who do well and also those who feel stuck.

If it seems useful, at the end discuss how well the group has worked together and what group members think could have been done differently. Then ask: 'What do you think you have learned from this activity that can be applied in future activities?'

This activity can be done with any number of people up to about 16. The more people there are, the more difficult it is to do the task. An alternative if there is a large number of people is to have two separate groups, perhaps with some friendly competition between the two groups.

Warning: This activity involves close physical contact and may be best introduced after the group has done a few other activities. Be especially aware of the hazards of this exercise if working with clients who are likely to have been abused.

Objectives

This activity encourages team building and group formation. It involves trust, persistence and problem solving. Above all, it encourages creative team solutions.

Removals

Materials needed

Whatever large natural objects that are available. These could include logs and large stones that the team might decide to use as stepping-stones.

Instructions

The group of people has to move from one specified spot of the forest to another without carrying anyone or touching the ground. They need to ensure that any participants who are weaker or have disabilities are helped to achieve the task. The team is allowed 10 minutes to discuss together how they will do this and to collect any items they might need. These could be left conveniently nearby, depending on the group's ability.

When the team is ready, they start the process. If anyone slips off a log or stone, you might have a rule that they have to go back two or three paces or some similar rule. Make sure that everyone in the group is being used for the task and is listened to.

If you have a large number of participants you could split them into small groups. Get them to discuss in their own groups for 10 minutes. Then all the teams go at the same time so that they can't copy each other's technique.

Observe how the participants decide how they are going to do the task. Be aware of those who are passive and those who attempt to control the others.

Once they have finished, you may wish to discuss with the team/s what the activity was like for them and especially how they felt individually about their part in the discussion before they started.

Objectives

This is a game about communication, relationship building and trust. It is fun and also challenging.

Broomstick obstacles

Materials needed

One or more brooms. Avoid very heavy brooms that can hurt if they fall on people's heads.

Instructions

This activity involves balancing a broom in the air, with the handle on an open hand or a single finger. The person then walks through an obstacle course of natural objects placed on the ground.

Get the group to plan the obstacle course. It can be made even more difficult by doing it in a forest where low branches of trees could be additional obstacles for the unwary participant.

Once the course is built, one person balances the broom and the other group members give instructions such as forward, left and right. It is important to ensure that everyone in the group is included in helping the person with instructions as it is difficult, if not impossible, to do this successfully without everyone helping.

You may want to have a team competition, timing each person's effort and deducting 10 seconds or so every time the broom is dropped.

Objectives

This exercise involves trust, listening to instructions, balance, taking responsibility and caring for the person with the broomstick. It encourages team-building and group participation.

Simple abseil

Materials needed

A length of strong rope.

Instructions

This activity involves using a rope to get the whole group of participants safely down a very steep part of a hill.

Find a steep, grassy hill free of loose rocks (scree). Avoid cliffs or hills that lead to cliff edges at the bottom. Attach a rope securely at the top of the hill to a large tree or solid rock. If you are working with a large group, divide the group into teams, with each team containing people of different sizes, ages and abilities.

Tell the teams that their goal is to get everyone in the team down safely while holding the rope and going backwards, as if they were abseiling.

The teams need to ensure that even the smallest and least able member gets down safely. They need to decide how to achieve this. Ideas you could suggest if they get stuck include pairing a small person above with a bigger person just below or people at the front giving instructions to those above them. They could also agree not to go too fast.

Once you are completely satisfied that they can achieve the task safely for all the team members, let them begin their abseil.

Talk about the experience after they have all finished. Focus especially on what it was like to consider the needs of the smallest/least able team members.

Objectives

This activity promotes and encourages team building, working together, cooperation, responsibility and caring for others. It also may help some clients face and conquer their fear of heights or learn to trust the rest of the team.

Survival

Introduction

Surviving in the most hostile of conditions, with the minimum of resources, is a fundamental desire common to most people.

Babies are born totally dependent on their primary carer – usually mother – for survival. Yet within a few short years the young child is building dens at the bottom of the garden or wanting to camp out in a field.

Later in childhood and right into adult life that desire is often satisfied through learning how others survive. Earlier generations devoured stories about survival such as *Robinson Crusoe* and *Huckleberry Finn.* More recently TV has satisfied that desire by showing celebrities surviving on desert islands and families agreeing to give up all electronic distractions for a week or more.

Survival experts Ray Mears and Bear Grylls have both captured the attention of a whole generation with their UK TV programmes showing survival in extremes ranging from hostile deserts to bleak arctic regions. Millions around the world are enthralled by how they can build a boat from a tree trunk, capture ugly creatures and turn them into tasty snacks and find drinking water in the centre of a jungle branch. Yet most people watching will never have the need actually to do any of these things for survival.

This inbuilt fascination for survival can be harnessed to help emotionally troubled clients to learn about emotional self-care and to build confidence in their abilities.

Ken Griffiths believes the will to survive is key to the fight against wind, cold, wet and heat. He writes: 'Once you have found the will to survive, your main aids to survival are inner strength, knowledge, the equipment you have or can find or manufacture, and your psychological approach. This latter is greatly enhanced by a sense of humour' (Griffiths, 2007, page 9).

Showing clients survival skills and encouraging them to experiment with survival can develop their inner strength and boost their psychological resilience.

Make a fire

Materials needed

Magnifying glass or two flint rocks or flint-and-steel firelighter (available from camping and outdoor shops). As a last resort, a box of matches or cigarette lighter. Also a fold-up shovel (from outdoor stores) and water to put out the fire.

Instructions

In most areas of the world a fire is essential for survival, and this activity involves showing clients the way to light one in the wilds and keep it lit for cooking, heat and protection from wild animals.

Find a suitable place to light a fire. Fires in national forests are strictly forbidden in most countries – and for good reason. An open field away from trees or a rocky place near a river or stream may be best. Explain what you are looking for, including the reasons why a forest is not the right place, and get the participants to find a suitable spot. Encourage them to clear the area completely of all combustible material. In a grassy area they can use the shovel to cut a rectangular turf and put it face down on the grass. Then they can scoop out some soil and put it on top of the turf. When they have finished they can put the soil back and return the turf, leaving the area as they found it.

Instead of using paper, get the people to gather some tinder. This is material that is used to start the fire. Dry leaves and grass can be used. So can some tree barks such as birch bark, which peels off like paper. The lining of an empty bird's nest can also be used. They will need about a football-size worth of tinder.

Then they need lots of kindling. This is very small dead twigs, none thicker than a pencil, and pieces of bark. They will need about three times the amount of kindling than tinder.

Finally, they can gather large pieces of wood to keep the fire going. Explain that some woods burn better than others. Any woods with a soft white centre (such as alder) or are still living are very difficult to burn. Others such as pines flare up and then are quickly gone. The best woods for this stage are dry deciduous woods such as oak, birch and hawthorn.

Once everything is gathered, the participants arrange a small pyramid of tinder mixed with kindling, leaving a gap underneath for the air to get to. Then they can begin lighting the fire. This can be done by directing the sun's rays on to the pyramid using a magnifying glass or creating a spark using flints or flint-and-steel. Once the pile starts to smoke they need to blow on it carefully until the fire catches. Then add more tinder and kindling until there is a large, consistent flame. Only then do they start adding large wood.

If the participants can't get the flame to work, consider having ready some paper and matches or a cigarette lighter. Encourage them to keep persisting until they succeed. After you are finished, put out the fire with water, making sure that the embers are cold. Then cover up all evidence of the fire.

Objectives

Make a Fire encourages initiative and hopefully achievement. It promotes safe ways of lighting fire and preserving nature. It can satisfy the child-like desire of most people, adults included, to play with fire but in a safe environment.

Water in the wild

Materials needed

Some old clear plastic bottles. Purifying tablets and, if possible, filter straws (available from outdoor shops).

Instructions

With the participants, explore ways in which they could survive in the wild through finding water that was safe to drink.

Explain to them that water is vital for life. An adult in an emergency can survive for many days or even weeks without food, but will start the process of dying after just three days without water. Each person needs at least a litre of water a day to stay healthy. In hot areas this increases to two or more litres a day.

Get the clients to imagine that they are lost in the area of the outdoors where you are based. How will they find water? There may be a river or stream nearby. How will they know the water is pure? They might look for springs where the water is coming out of the side of the hill. This is one of the safest forms of water. A stream may have had animals drinking from it and polluting it.

If there is no obvious source of water in the area, see if people can trace some sources of water by watching birds and insects, which both depend on a water source (though not necessarily a pure one) for survival. Follow a line of ants to see where their water source is. Watch how birds are flying. If they are flying fast and low in one direction, that may be where their water source is. If the participants notice birds flying from branch to branch, they may be full of water, having just visited the water source.

If someone was out in the wild and needing water, the person could gather rain water or water from dew. How would they do that?

Once sources of water have been located, fill the old plastic bottles with samples of the water and look at them carefully. Would the samples be safe to drink in an emergency? Show people the filter straws and purifying tablets. Ask them if the samples could be made drinkable with purifying tablets or would they need filtering as well? Filtering could be done through a teeshirt or even a sock. Explain that without purifying tablets only by boiling clear water for 15 minutes will it be safe to drink. Any less could be dangerous.

Warning: This is an exploratory exercise. Unless you know the water is 100 per cent safe, do not let the participants drink it.

Objectives

This activity promotes self-care and a sense of achievement. Finding new sources of water and considering how to make the water safe enhances creativity and a sense of achievement. Searching for water together helps with building the group in a positive way.

Build a shelter

Materials needed

Some no-water antiseptic hand wash. A snack and drink or a picnic lunch.

Instructions

This is an exercise in which you and the clients explore making forest shelters.

When you are in a forested area, start by getting the participants to discuss where it would be suitable to build a shelter and where it would be unsuitable. For instance, it may be important to choose the driest spot, sheltered from strong winds and not where water will run when it rains.

Once they have discussed the best kind of area, it is time to get the clients to explore various potential places to build a shelter. This may take some trial and error until they are all satisfied. Warn people to avoid areas where there may be an abundance of ants that sting.

The next step is to decide the kind of shelter needed. The easiest by far for one person is to make a thick pile of dry leaves, bark and pine needles and wriggle into it as if it were a sleeping bag. The clients may want to try this. Once they have prepared their shelter and tried it out, ask them: Will it keep you warm and dry? (Probably.) Is it comfortable? (Probably not.) What are the disadvantages of this kind of shelter? (Nowhere to sit in the dry, getting covered in insects while asleep.)

Another kind of shelter is built around a fallen tree or one that has been cut down. Instead of everyone making their own shelter, get them to find a side of the trunk where everyone can sit down. Then they can find some branches to lean against the fallen tree to keep out the wind. They then cover the branches with leaves, bark, twigs or pine needles to keep the rain out.

Instead of a fallen tree participants might choose a large rock. Again, lean branches at an angle against the rock and cover the branches with whatever can be found. The next stage is to make a bed in the shelter. Clients decide what to use for the bed. They could consider dry leaves.

Once people have built their shelter everyone (including you) can squeeze inside, sit down, wash hands with antiseptic hand wash and enjoy a snack or lunch together. It will probably be an unforgettable experience.

This is an exercise only. The shelter initially built will probably not be suitable for sleeping in overnight. But it does not stop you discussing what it would be like to sleep there. How could clients ensure they are safe? (Checking what local hazards there might be. In the UK, for instance, the problem might be rain in the night. In Romania, potential hazards could include bears, wolves and wild boar as well as adders.)

Objectives

Build a Shelter will give participants a feeling of immense achievement and a positive sense of self-satisfaction. If it is done within a group it can assist with group formation and team development. Building a shelter can also be seen as a parallel to building confidence.

Finding your way

Materials needed

Compass, local map (or any map, if a local map is not easily available).

Instructions

This is an exercise in which participants explore various ways in which they could navigate in the countryside, forest or mountains. It can be done without moving from the spot and is not intended as a full navigational exercise.

Start by opening a map and getting people to see if they can find the sign for North on it. In most countries this is indicated at the side of the map with an arrow and the letter N. Then show them the compass and ask them to point out North on it. Ask: How can you use the compass and the map to find North from where you are standing? (They put the compass on the map with the compass North pointing in the same direction as the map's North. Then they move the map and compass around until the needle is directly on North.)

Once they find North they can look at the map and decide which direction they need to go. If they were to get lost or stuck in fog they could use the compass to keep going in the direction they decided.

Ask them how they could find their way using a map without a compass. (From a high spot they could look for prominent landscape features – river, forest, church spire, hill or mountain. Then they point the symbols on the map at those features and they have a rough idea of direction.) If there was no map or compass available, how could they find their direction of travel? (In the Northern Hemisphere the sun points South at midday.)

Get people to explore forest trees and vegetation to see if there is any difference. If they find that one side grows algae or moss and the other doesn't ask them which side could be South and which North. (North is likely to be colder and damper in the Northern Hemisphere so algae and/or moss may tend to grow on that side.)

They may also notice that trees and vegetation, particularly in exposed areas where there are few hills or mountains, tend to bend in a particular direction. The direction they are bending towards indicates the direction of the prevailing wind. If you can find out in advance which direction the prevailing wind generally comes from in the area (through weather forecasts or via the internet), you can tell the direction.

An optional extra for this exercise is to prepare in advance a simple map to follow using the ideas learned. You could get people to find a particular spot where there is some 'treasure' you have hidden under a tree.

Objectives

This exercise can build participants' confidence and self-esteem as they learn to find their way through direction. Cooperating together to search for clues to direction by studying the trees can help with teambuilding.

Self-care

Materials needed

A rucksack and an assortment of items that might or might not be useful for survival (take advice on survival gear from your local outdoor shop).

Instructions

This is an exercise in which you as a group look at items that could be useful for survival in the wild.

Start by displaying the rucksack and the assortment of items. Get the clients to choose what they think needs to go in the rucksack and what they can manage without.

Items that would be dubious for survival could include chewing gum, nail brush, hair dryer, ornament and face flannel. Items that may make the difference between life and death could include waterproof coat, spare sweater, spare socks, Mars bar, drink, piece of string, spare shoelace, pen, paper, mobile phone, map, compass, whistle, torch, survival bag, waterproof matches, thermal blanket.

Once the items have been identified and discussed you may want to explore signalling. See if the participants can identify the three most useful items for this – mobile phone, torch and whistle. Mobile phones often have poor reception in wild areas so the other two items might be more useful. In most countries in the world, a distress signal consists of three whistle blasts or three flashes of a torch, repeated each minute. In the UK this changes to six signals repeated each minute. In the Alps, the rule is six signals spread over a minute, and the sign of rescuers is three signals over a minute. If you are in the countryside, mountains or forests, do *not* practice the signals as it could cause a false alarm!

You might want to discuss how to prevent cold and damp. Ask the participants what from the rucksack they could use if they were lost and getting cold at night, for instance. Hopefully they will identify the coat and sweater. They might also indicate the thermal blanket and survival bag. Ask: Why do you think the survival bag is orange? (To make it easily identified by rescuers, including a helicopter.) How do they think a very thin thermal blanket can keep a person warm? (The silvery surface reflects back body heat so it is not lost and also protects from wind and rain.) Participants may want to try out the survival bag, which goes over the head and right down to the ground. If they try the thermal blanket it will be difficult to pack it small again.

You could also think about wild animals and other possible dangers. Get them to identify local dangers and suggest ways of protecting themselves from them.

Objectives

This is an exercise in physical self-care, and as such it can enhance emotional self-care and self-esteem.

Food from the wild

Materials needed

A book or two on edible food from the wild such as *Food for Free* (Mabey, 1972/2007). Antiseptic no-water hand wash and some tissues.

Instructions

This is an ideal activity for the summer/autumn when there is an abundance of fruit. Invite participants to imagine that they are lost in the wild and have to find ways of surviving. They then collect berries, nuts, flowers and leaves that they think could be eaten. They can also use their sense of smell to detect food that is edible and things that might be poisonous or unpleasant to eat.

This activity works well when combined with a walk in the countryside. Before you set out ask people: 'What various things can you smell and taste in nature?' Acknowledge their ideas, even those that seem a little far-fetched! Invite them to use their sense of smell as they walk along and also consider what may be edible.

Warning: If you are working with young children, be aware that they are quite readily put things in their mouths and eat what looks pretty without giving it much thought. It is essential therefore that you have a firm contract with them that they do not taste anything at all from nature without checking first with an adult. This is probably similar to what parents/carers have already told them

There is a wide variety of smells in nature. Some can be sensed from a distance. For instance, clients might observe the general damp, musty smell of the thick forest or the strong smell of fresh animal droppings. Other smells can be found only by getting close up to, say, flowers, leaves and fungi. Discuss the smells that people find. Are the smells strong or subtle, pleasant or nasty? Many animals rely on their sense of smell to find food and avoid danger. Participants may like to become 'tracker dogs' – following a route using their sense of smell. There may be a general smell in the air and the 'tracker dogs' can track it down to a particular spot, then show it to the rest of the group.

Tastes in nature vary according to the geographical area and the time of year. Spring is a good time to taste the sweet pith of certain grasses. Summer provides early fruit (such as wild strawberry) and the pollen and nectar of flowers such as honeysuckle. Autumn and Winter are the best times to taste berries (blackberries, wild raspberries), seeds and nuts such as hazel, sweet chestnut and walnut. Get people to try some bitter tasting fruit such as elderberry, crab apple and sloe. Talk about the tastes. Are they pleasant or unpleasant? Sweet or sour? Do they leave an aftertaste? Would they be foods they would eat if they were lost in the wild?

Warning: Get participants to wash their hands using no-water hand wash before each tasting session. Avoid tasting fungi unless you are an expert. Many fungi are deadly poisonous. If you are in doubt about the identity of a fruit, break it open and touch it to the outside of your lip. If it stings, then it is probably poisonous. If not, taste it with the end of your tongue before putting it in your mouth. Only let people taste it when you are completely satisfied that it is safe.

Objectives

Sensory acuity in nature involves not just seeing, hearing and touching, but smell and taste, too (see Appendix 1). Clients who have been abused or traumatised in other ways may have lost some of their sensory ability. This activity can be a fun way to help them begin to recover it. The 'tracker dog' activity will appeal to hyperactive young people. Tasting wild fruit, even with a clear contract to check with a knowledgeable person first, will be a new experience for many of the participants. Such permission-giving can be quite liberating for people who have repressed their creative spirit and sense of adventure.

Get the message

Materials needed

None. Items used will be natural ones found locally.

Instructions

In this exercise the participants imagine that they are lost in the wilderness and searching for water or food. How will they leave natural signs for others to find and rescue them?

Start by asking people to come up with ideas for marking the direction they are going. They might suggest arrows or markers on the ground or on the trees. How can they make these arrows or marks? If there is chalk around, it could be marked on the trees. Small stones or twigs could be made into arrows. A branch could be used to mark arrows or markers on the ground.

Once they have come up with a range of ideas, split them into two groups and get each group to mark a path in different directions from where you are standing. Once they have finished they come back to the centre and each group attempts to follow the other group's signals.

Discuss afterwards what the experience was like. Would rescuers have been able to find them if they had used those markers?

Objectives

This is a useful exercise in nonverbal communication, teamwork and self-care. It will be particularly effective for clients who have low confidence yet who come up with ideas.

Cooking food outside

Materials needed

Aluminium foil, kitchen roll and no-water antiseptic hand wash. Paper plates. Sugar and margarine if needed. One knife for spreading margarine on toast. A sharp knife for preparing cooking sticks. Water to sprinkle on the fire or to put out flames on the cooking sticks. Whatever foods participants decide they can cook (see below).

Instructions

This exercise can be linked with the activity Make a Fire. It involves people in preparing and cooking food on a fire that they have lit, without using any pans or shop-bought cooking utensils.

Start by asking the clients what food they want to cook and what cooking techniques would be suitable for this exercise. Ideas might include potatoes and/or root vegetables wrapped in aluminium foil and put in embers, bread or marshmallows toasted on sticks, bananas or apples baked in foil or on sticks and sprinkled with sugar. They might want to make their own bread using dough wrapped several times around a stick.

Once the decisions are made it is time to prepare the utensils. Cooking sticks are best made from thin straight branches that are living (green). Dry ones will catch fire too easily. Use a sharp knife to cut the branch, then peel off the bark, leaves and buds using the knife.

The fire itself needs to have been burning for some time and the flames to have died down. You will then have a bed of hot grey embers. The food wrapped in foil can be buried in this (using two strong sticks, or oven gloves if you have them), then pulled out when ready (about 30 minutes depending on the fire). They need leaving for about two minutes before attempting to unwrap them. The sticks with food on need holding a few centimetres above the embers and turned constantly. The temptation is to put them into the embers, but this will burn the food.

Make sure people use hand wash before eating the food. They can use the paper plates or eat direct from the foil or sticks. Delicious!

Warning: It is best to avoid meat products because they could cause illness if not cooked thoroughly or if carried around raw for a long time without refrigeration.

Objectives

Being able to cook food on an open fire without utensils is a major achievement and a cause for celebration. The potatoes might be hard and the toast burned, but most people will be thrilled with their success. This exercise builds confidence and emphasises self-care.

Confidence

Introduction

Clients often need confidence. This does not depend on academic achievement or ability. Rather, it is measured in how fulfilled people are in their lives. Are they content and satisfied? Or are they constantly doing themselves down with negative self-comments?

Sadly, so often today people of all ages say negative things about themselves: 'I'm no good.' 'Everyone's better at doing things than me.' 'Maybe other people are cleverer than me.' 'I don't feel special.'

Confidence-building activities in the outdoors can change negatives into positives. 'I'm all right – and so are others.' 'I can succeed in doing things.' 'I'm clever at some things and other people are clever at other things.' 'I'm special!'

Skill in the outdoors, while sometimes thought of as natural or even God-given, is a quality that needs learning. Cashmore describes three forms of skill: motor skills; perceptual (sensing or environmental) skills; and cognitive (thinking) skills. 'Skill is made possible by a person's aptitude and builds on their ability,' he says (Cashmore, 2002, page 234).

Confidence could be seen as a very individual thing. But the confidence each person has also affects other people around him or her. For instance, if I feel good about myself I am more likely to feel good about others and this will have a knock-on effect. If I hate myself, I may either think other people are no good or, in comparison, they are much better than me. This in turn affects them.

Berne (1962) explained that every individual has certain beliefs about himself and others (additions overleaf are from Boholst, 2002):

I'm OK – I like myself; I'm proud of what I do
I'm not OK – I don't feel good about me; I wish I hadn't been born
You're OK – Most people can be trusted; I find it easy to like others
You're not OK – I distrust people; I wish some people were dead

These beliefs can be grouped into four Life Positions:

I'm OK; you're OK – healthy position
I'm OK; you're not OK – paranoid position
I'm not OK; you're OK – depressive position
I'm not OK; you're not OK – futility position

Therapeutic adventure activities can give participants the confidence to move from one of the negative positions to the healthy position.

Exploring in the dark

Materials needed

Torch for the facilitator and any other helpers.

Instructions

Exploring in the dark has an element of both scare and excitement. It is best done after doing the easier Night Walk activity.

If possible, choose a starry night to do this activity. Make sure that participants have suitable clothes on for warmth and in case it rains. Stand in the dark until everyone can start to see. This is known as getting your night vision. Then go for a walk that is familiar to you during the day. (You might want to go back with the group in the morning so they can see what it looks like in the light.) Use your torch to guide the way, if you need to. At regular intervals get people to stop. Then switch off any torches and ask them to become aware of what they can see and hear.

For adults and older young people you could consider using the stars to find directions. In the Northern Hemisphere the Pole Star points the way North (see Google pictures). From there people can work out other directions.

In the summer you could lie in a field and look at the stars together. Then, while you are in the field, get people to draw the position of the stars on pieces of paper. Be aware that there may be dew on the grass. Use a groundsheet or blanket if you prefer.

Objectives

Exploring in the Dark enables participants to learn new skills of finding their way in the dark. It will help them to be confident in what could be a scary situation.

Swaying branch

Materials needed

None.

Instructions

Swaying Branch is a team exercise in which one person (the Branch) sways back and forth as if blown by the wind while the rest of the group in a circle keep the Branch from falling over.

This activity is intended for a group that is already functioning together well. If you are working with a large group, divide them into teams of about eight. It is best done on a soft area such as grass or a clear forest floor in case someone falls over. Although it is a lot of fun, the important part of it is learning to trust others as well as looking after and caring for each other. Without this care there could be injuries, physical and even psychological.

Start by explaining to the participants the correct position to take when they are in the group circle. This involves standing with one foot in front of the other, arms stretched out, elbows locked and fingers loose and flexible. Each group member must be ready and alert all the time.

The group members need to be shoulder to shoulder, with arms outstretched ready. In this position their hands will almost touch the person standing in the middle. Gradually the group can move back to allow for more swaying. Make sure large and small people are distributed evenly through the group to avoid weak points in the circle.

Next, demonstrate how to be the Branch. This involves keeping feet together and closing eyes. The Branch crosses his or her arms with hands on opposite shoulders. This gives protection. The bottom is tightened and the body is kept straight.

It is important before the Branch starts to sway back and forth that the Branch establishes a contract with the rest of the group. A contract is 'an explicit bilateral commitment to a well-defined course of action' (Berne, 1966/1994, page 362). Before they start, Branch and group contract together:

Branch: 'I'm ready to sway. Are you ready to catch me?'

Group: 'We're ready to catch you. Sway away.'

Branch: 'Swaying.'

The Branch sways and is passed around the group for as long as he or she wants. When the Branch has had enough, it is a simple matter of opening eyes, standing up and thanking the group.

Then another person volunteers as the Branch until everyone in the group who wants to has had a turn.

Discuss the activity after everyone has finished. How supported did people feel? Instead of asking for verbal feedback, consider asking them to hold up fingers to show how much out of 10 they felt supported. If a person (or more than one person) didn't feel very supported, consider how to deal with this in the group.

Objectives

This exercise is a gentle but challenging activity to build real trust between people and confidence in people's abilities. It emphasises concentration and team work. Above all it is a beautiful blend of excitement and scare.

Scream away

Materials needed

None.

Instructions

This brief but fun activity involves everyone finding a place in the wild away from other people and at a given signal screaming loudly.

Every human reaches a point occasionally when he or she feels like screaming. This activity gives clients the confidence to do this in a way that is fun and safe. Explain to the participants that they are going to be given a chance to release their bad feelings and leave them in the wild. This will involve making lots of noise, but no one will be affected in a bad way by it.

Get people to spread out, well away from each other and from other people enjoying the countryside. At a given signal (such as a whistle) everyone screams as loudly as possible for about a minute. The second signal brings the activity to the end. People then make their way back to you and, if appropriate, talk about the experience.

Some of them may complain about having a sore throat. This is likely to last for only a few minutes. Our experience is that allowing a release of (unspecified) bad feelings in this way more than compensates for a little discomfort for a few minutes.

Warning: Screaming at the top of your voice can be very releasing and it is tempting for people to do it regularly. If they live in a town or city and do this, the chances are that other people will hear them. Explain that it is only suitable when they are completely away from other people.

Objectives

Scream Away provides a major release of feelings and appropriate and safe expression of anger and other feelings. People who regularly release their bad feelings often feel more confident and relaxed than those who keep them bottled up.

Stepping across

Materials needed

Large stones occurring naturally near a stream or small river. A rope for safety if young children are involved.

Instructions

Stepping Across involves participants getting the whole group across a stream or small river safely and with dry feet, using only stepping stones.

Plan the crossing place in advance, making sure there are enough large moveable stones so that people can build their stepping stones. Remember that the depth of the water will vary according to the season, so do your advance checking as near to the actual event as possible.

Go together to the water and outline to the clients what the exercise involves. Together they are to find large stones (preferably free of slippery green algae), put them in the water and make the stepping stones across. Then they are to ensure that everyone gets across safely.

The temptation will often be for the confident team members to cross the river quickly, leaving the others to struggle behind them. This is *not* the point of this exercise. It is about building the confidence of even the weakest member of the group.

Once the stepping stones are in place, ask the team how they will ensure that the youngest and least able group members will get across. Listen to their ideas rather than tell them what to do. They might suggest holding hands, carrying smaller ones or using the rope as a handrail for any children.

When you are completely satisfied that they can complete the task, let them do it. Afterwards, you might decide to discuss what it was like working as a team. How did the more able participants handle the responsibility? What was it like for those who may have been fearful?

Warning: Cancel this activity if there has been recent heavy rain. Small streams and rivers can become dangerous torrents with little or no warning.

Objectives

This is an exercise in group effort, caring for self and others, cooperation and confidence building.

Tricky situation

Materials needed

None.

Instructions

Tricky Situation involves creative thinking and discussion about possible difficult situations and how participants could handle them. It is an ideal activity around a campfire or while relaxing in a field.

When people are comfortable, explain that you are going to give an imaginary difficulty and want to know how they would respond. If you are working with a group, it could become a team effort. They then make sure that everyone contributes to the ideas. Here are a few situations, though you may prefer to use your own:

A young man gets his foot stuck in a rabbit hole and strains his ankle. He can't walk on his own. What can the rest of the group do?

The group have an argument about which way to go. You don't want to split up. What do you do?

You are on a walk and it is lunchtime. You discover that the people carrying lunch have eaten half of it already. What do you say and do?

A group member with outdoor clothes on goes exploring down a hole between two rocks and gets stuck. He can't get out again and is starting to panic. How can you help?

A young woman finds a baby rabbit near a series of rabbit holes. She wants to take it home as a pet. How do you persuade her it needs to stay in the wild with its family?

One of the group falls into a very large patch of nettles and is covered with red rash. What can you do to help him or her feel better until you get home?

If necessary, facilitate the discussion. For instance, in the case of the man who has strained his ankle you might suggest that the group uses an item of clothing to support his ankle. Then get them to try it out on a volunteer. The person stuck in the hole may need to remove some clothes in order to be helped out. (We suggest it is not necessary to practise this one!) The person covered in nettle rash may benefit from dock leaves. Ask participants to search for some.

Objectives

This exercise helps to give people confidence in knowing what to do in tricky situations. Talking about the situations and coming up with ideas can also build their confidence. Finding ways to care for others can enhance clients' empathic understanding.

Confidence booster

Materials needed

None.

Instructions

This activity involves dividing the group into two or more teams. Each team plans an assault course using natural materials and then helps the other team successfully to complete the course.

Find an area of the forest where there are plenty of fallen trees, rocks or other obstacles. Start by explaining that an assault course was originally designed for soldiers to practise on and to build their strength for getting over or under difficult objects. In this case each team is designing an assault course and then helping the other team have the confidence to go through the course safely.

You might want to set each team limits for where they can design their course or simply let them use their creative imaginations. Be around to guide and advise them, especially if they want to incorporate very difficult or impossible tasks.

If they run out of ideas, they might consider the following:

Climb up one side and down the other of a thick fallen tree trunk or large rock
Crawl through a small gap between a horizontal tree or rock and the ground
Squeeze between two trees that are growing very close together
Cross a muddy ditch too wide to jump over
Find their way through a thick group of saplings

As a variation, consider getting the participants to design an assault course for you and any other leaders involved. Then get them to facilitate you to complete the course. If there are parts of the course that you are uncertain about, get the participants to demonstrate how to conquer them. If you are still uncertain, say this to the participants and don't attempt those parts. Your admission that you can't do everything may well be a huge confidence boost to the team members.

Objectives

This is an excellent way to build clients' confidence and help them to feel good about themselves. It is also an important way to emphasise self-care and care for others.

Finding your way up

Materials needed

None.

Instructions

In this exercise participants are encouraged to climb a steep rocky or grass-covered hill without ropes or climbing gear.

Choose a steep hill with plenty of rocks for handholds. Alternatively, find a grassy slope that is very steep. Avoid vertical cliffs as climbing these would almost certainly be dangerous without specialist knowledge and equipment. Check out the hill yourself or get someone with more experience to check it out for you to make sure that it is suitable and reasonably safe. Be aware that what is perfectly safe on a dry day may be dangerous when wet or in frosty conditions.

Start by explaining the importance of using hands and feet in the climb. The key is to have three points of contact at all times – two hands and a foot or two feet and a hand. Encourage participants to practise this before actually starting the climb.

For the climb itself, you could get people to climb individually or you might consider them following each other up, stopping together at suitable places along the route. If you use the latter approach, make sure they are far enough apart so that heads and faces are not kicked by the person up ahead. Also get people to shout out loudly if a stone or rock starts falling so that those below are not hit by it.

Be prepared to give plenty of encouragement to the participants who are hesitant at first and yet who make it to the top.

A more advanced option for is to descend by the same route. This must be done in the same way as descending a ladder – facing the rocks and using hands and feet.

Objectives

Finding Your Way Up is a good exercise for building clients' confidence in their ability. Experience has shown that it is often the smaller or apparently less able clients who excel in this activity. Even people who 'freeze' partly up the hill can gain confidence as they are coaxed by other group members to go a little further.

Reach for the sky

Materials needed

A length of rope.

Instructions

The facilitator prepares this exercise in advance. Tie the rope tightly to a high, strong branch of a stout tree (or get someone else to do it for you). Leave one end dangling down out of reach of everyone, but not too high.

The object of the exercise is to reach for the sky, leaping up as high as possible to grab the rope and then swing on it. If you are working with a group, get each group member to have a turn, then go around again, this time getting them to put in more effort to make the leap. This is helped when team members shout encouragement to the person whose turn it is.

When everyone has succeeded (with, of course, suitable praise each time someone manages to grab the rope), try raising the rope slightly higher and see who can do it. If someone has not managed to reach the rope, get the team to come up with creative ideas for building the person's confidence sufficiently to succeed. Ideas could include bending very low and springing off the feet, or getting a slight boost from a stronger team member, who gently pushes the person's waist as he/she jumps. The important thing is to make sure that everyone succeeds.

Warning: This is not an easy task because the rope is free-swinging. Make sure that there are no dangerous obstacles beneath the tree that could injure a person who falls. Get people to practise jumping off a wall or other height and bending their knees as they hit the ground. This can cushion the impact of a fall. Also warn them that if they fall sideways, they must not put out their arm to break their fall. Instead, use both arms by their sides to cushion the fall by gently hitting the ground just before impact.

Objectives

The purpose of Reach for the Sky is to build clients' confidence in their own ability. By being more confident in themselves they are less likely to be intimidated by others. A client who is poor at socialising skills yet who achieves in this exercise will have a major boost of confidence that could well impact on the rest of his/her life.

Risk taking

Introduction

Risk is an important part of being healthy emotionally. Ellis Cashmore believes that 'we can become too secure and lose what has been historically a vital, heroic trait' (Cashmore, 2002, page 225). While society in general is becoming increasingly safety-conscious, extreme and highly-dangerous sports such as base-jumping, mountain running or skiing down cliffs (Xtreme skiing) are providing for people what is often missing in an over-safe society. Children, too, need to take risks, hopefully ones that are reasonably safe.

In today's super-safe society, children are overprotected by parents and society. In extreme cases they are escorted and protected 100 per cent of the time and never learn to think or make decisions for themselves. For generations, children have explored the world around them, climbed trees and taken risks. Minor falls and near misses enable them to learn how to make decisions. Without that, when children become adults they are sometimes afraid even to go out on their own.

Veteran mountaineer Malcolm Slesser, whose adventuring started at the age of 11, writes: 'For an enterprise to be called adventurous all that is needed is for the outcome to be unknowable' (Slesser, 2004, page 28). He writes that safety lies 'not in avoiding risk, but being aware of all the factors in play . . . Mothers of young children exhibit this awareness to an uncanny degree, in some cases so much as to inhibit the development of their offspring. It's a different choice to let the emerging child find for him or herself that safety lies in awareness of danger' (Slesser, 2004, page 14).

Providing opportunities in the wilds for people of all ages to take reasonably safe and carefully planned risks enables them to face their fears and overcome difficult situations in day-to-day life.

'The use of risk-recreation activities . . . provides an intervention that allows the individual freedom to make choices. For the participant who has experienced repeated failure, taking part in a successful activity contradicts their old beliefs and reinforces the new behaviour that enabled them to participate despite the uncertainty' (Wilderness Program, 2008).

Crossing the water

Materials needed

A length of rope. Participants are advised to wear swimming costumes or shorts with two or three warm top layers. Gym shoes (plimsoles/pumps/sneakers) or wetsuit shoes will give a reasonable grip. Ensure that everyone can change into dry trousers, socks and shoes soon after the activity.

Instructions

When done properly, crossing a river on foot can be highly adventurous and exciting. With inadequate preparation, however, it can be one of the most dangerous activities possible.

Choose a section of the river where the water is fairly shallow (less than knee deep for beginners) for about 10 metres along its length. Check it out in advance, walking back and forth through the water to make sure there are no deep pools. If possible, consult local experts about the part of the river you have chosen.

There are two ways to ensure that participants get across safely. If you are working with people with almost no experience of the outdoors, the first option is probably preferable. Tie a rope between two trees across the river, at or slightly below the smallest person's waist height. They then cross one at a time, holding the rope with both hands and keeping on the side of the rope upstream of the river flow. That way, if a person slips, there is more chance of avoiding being washed down by the river. If you have concerns, you or a helper could wait in the water downstream in case by remote chance someone is washed down by the current.

The second way to cross – and undoubtedly the most adventurous – involves holding the rope in both hands and crossing the river together, forming a V-shape much like geese fly when they are migrating. This involves a lot of teamwork and it is strongly recommended that the participants practice on dry land before making the crossing.

Choose a flat area such as a field or car park. Arrange people so that the two largest and strongest are at either end of the rope. The third strongest is in the middle and the others are spread evenly either side of the middle person. Everyone holds the rope firmly in both hands. The two at each end act as anchors, holding the rope tight, a bit like the anchor person in a tug-of-war.

The middle person moves forward slowly. As he or she does so, the rest of the group move slightly towards the centre, always keeping the rope taut. The next two then start moving forward, and so on until the V-shape is formed. Keep moving forward, ensuring that the rope is always taut and the V-shape is maintained.

Participants go through the same process for the actual crossing. It is really important that all group members think safety for themselves and others all the time in this exercise. Once they have reached the other side they need to get dry and warm again. This is not an exercise to stand around talking after the event.

When everyone is warm, dry and possibly indoors, ask what it was like for them. How safe did they feel? What did they need to do to overcome their fear? What was it like thinking of others? How do they feel now?

Severe warning: Cancel this exercise completely if there has been any recent rain. Rivers can quickly swell to torrents after rain, with sometimes lethal consequences.

Objectives

This exercise is an excellent way to help clients to take a big risk and at the same time emphasise to them the importance of safety. Encouraging clients to think of others as well as themselves helps with teambuilding and working together.

Rock clambering

Materials needed

Participants will need shop-bought or home-made hiking sticks for stability as well as a change of socks.

Instructions

Clambering over river rocks may sound easy, but there are hazards and risks along the route. The idea of this exercise is to get from one point to another over rocks without slipping off or ending up in the water.

Find a riverbed where the rocks are fairly close together and relatively free of slippery green moss. Choose a route in advance and check it out to ensure reasonable safety. The route may be better along one side of the river rather than across it.

When the clients do the rock clambering they may well find it easier to use a stick to assist in jumping from rock to rock. Remember if you are working with young children that they may find the jumps too long and may need some assistance. This is an exercise in caring for self and thinking of others. Suggest that the stronger, more able participants consider those who are not so strong and assist them.

Be prepared for a few wet feet if clients slip as they cross from one rock to the other.

After people have finished the chosen route (and put on dry socks if necessary), you might consider having some discussion. Ask them what it was like clambering over the rocks. Did they find it scary or exciting – or both? What was it like helping other people who might be struggling?

Objectives

This mildly risk-taking activity can help clients conquer their fears and also encourage team-building through helping others. By taking care of themselves and being aware of others they have maintained an 'I'm OK, You're OK' Life Position (Berne 1972/1975).

Run in the dark

Materials needed

Blindfolds.

Instructions

Run in the Dark is a trust exercise that involves clients working in pairs, one blindfolded and one sighted. The pair start by walking, then eventually running at full speed together across a field.

First, make sure that everyone has done warm-ups and stretches so they are ready to run. Find a large, fairly flat area with soft ground such as grass or forest floor. Don't worry if there are a few mounds or lumps around. This makes the challenge even more fun.

Invite participants to find a partner and decide who will be blindfolded first. Now the two people hold hands, and the one without the blindfold guides his/her partner on a slow walk for two minutes. Call out or blow the whistle when the time has been reached. The next stage is spending two minutes walking at a normal pace. This changes to a fast walk for 30 seconds and a jog for 30 seconds. Finish with a run for 15 seconds, leading to a run at full speed for 15 seconds.

Give everyone time to relax and get their breath back. Then invite them to swap around and do the same again.

After finishing the exercise, invite some discussion. What was it like for people to trust someone else so completely? How did they feel?

Objectives

Run in the Dark is an exercise in building trust and confidence. It may be useful for clients whose trust has been violated in some kind of way in the past. People who have been abused may at first find the idea of being blindfolded very frightening. Taking things step by step may be necessary, but the extra time will be well worth it. This exercise will almost certainly lead to plenty of laughter.

Climb in the treetops

Materials needed

None.

Instructions

As children most of us loved climbing trees. Usually children will only climb as high as they feel confident, depending on their developmental age. This exercise is about encouraging participants to climb trees and then to experiment with taking a risk by going *even higher.*

As the facilitator, choose an area of forest where there are plenty of trees for climbing. Deciduous forest is probably better than coniferous because the latter tends to have very scratchy branches. Avoid trees that are dead or dying or that have a lot of rotten branches.

Invite the clients to climb a tree one at a time. Guidance from you and the others can help, though be aware that some people find such 'advice' annoying. When they hesitate, encourage them to go a bit further, always being aware of the client's reaction. If there are enough trees around, get the second person to climb another tree and so on until they are all high up in the treetops. Another option is to get participants to climb the same tree one at a time, joining each other in the treetop. If they can see around them, get them to call out what they can see.

Descending is a simple reversal of the order of climbing. Ensure that no one steps on the hand, head or face of someone below. After descending, the clients might want to talk about their experience of climbing in the treetops.

Warning: This exercise is only suitable in dry weather. Wet branches can be extremely and dangerously slippery. Watch carefully for rotten branches and if necessary warn people to avoid them.

Objectives

Clients who are willing to take the risk by going slightly higher than they feel confident will hopefully have a surge of pride in their achievement. The sense of elation from being high up in a tree you have climbed is hard to equal in any other activity. So often today's children are told to take care and avoid risks at all costs. Climb in the Treetops releases children's – and adults' – natural desire to climb and enjoy the experience.

Mud, glorious mud

Materials needed

Each participant will need a complete set of spare clothes (including socks and underclothing). For emergencies: rope and a large tree branch, ladder or wooden plank.

Instructions

Many adults recall as small children wanting to jump in mud puddles or play with mud and being told firmly: 'Don't get yourself [or your clothes] dirty.' This activity enables people of all ages to get completely covered in mud without any fear of comeback! The challenge is to cross an area of deep mud – walking, running or even swimming through it.

Find a wet, muddy area in the forest, near a river or across a marsh. It is important for safety to check how deep the mud is. This can easily be done by finding an assistant brave enough to walk across it in advance using a stick to check the depth at various points while crossing it.

Before you start, make sure you have safety equipment available. If someone gets into difficulty after sinking into the mud you could throw him or her a rope. You could instead use a tree branch, ladder or plank of wood for the person to crawl on. If you are working with young children, consider having the rope around the child's middle, tied using a nonslipping knot.

In addition, it is best to give clients some instructions and warnings. They have full permission to get completely muddy for this exercise. If they decide to wear shoes or trainers it is possible that they will lose one or both of them, so they need to go barefoot or risk losing their shoes. If they get into difficulty, the absolute worst thing to do is struggle to get out of the mud. It is far better to stretch across the surface of the mud, gently pulling their legs out and 'swimming' to a safer part.

There are various ways participants can get across the mud. You might suggest they all do it together, helping each other as they go. You might time each person as they cross the area individually. They could walk, then run, then crawl across, getting muddier each time they make the crossing. A photograph of the mud-covered person at the end of the exercise could be a treasure for each of them!

If there is a suitable area of woodland nearby, with separate areas for male and female, the participants could get changed into another set of old clothes outdoors before returning indoors to get a well-deserved shower.

Objectives

The permission to get completely muddy that comes with this activity will be a delight to many people. The risk-taking element can also be a way of overcoming a fear of sinking into mud that is often the subject of dreams. People who are initially hesitant about getting muddy may be the ones who end up the dirtiest!

Swing across

Materials needed

A length of rope.

Instructions

This favourite activity of children for countless generations (and now available for adults, too!) is achieved by tying a rope to a tree branch and using it to swing across a ditch or small stream.

Find a ditch where there is a good, stout branch of a tree located somewhere in the middle above the ditch. Choose a spot of the ditch where there is plenty of water or mud rather than rocks or tree stumps so that injuries as a result of any falls can be minimised. Tie the rope to the branch (or get a participant or helper to do it for you), making sure that it is secure enough to support the weight of the heaviest person. An alternative if the branch is high is to throw the rope over the branch and tie one end to a nearby tree. If you are working with young children, you might need to tie a knot in the rope to help them get a good grip on it.

At a given signal the person swings from one side of the ditch to the other, letting go in time to land on the other side. Clients need to reach up for the rope and tuck their legs up, bending their knees and lowering their legs at just the right moment. This will take some practice. If you are working with a group, you might consider challenging the whole group to get to the other side and back again, helping each other if necessary. Such help may be essential if the banks of the ditch are very steep and slippery.

Warning: The biggest danger, apart from falling, is kicking or bumping into someone on the other side. Take great care to ensure that team members keep clear of the swinging rope, with the facilitator only reaching out at the last moment to help the person land safely.

Objectives

Swing Across is a fun activity with plenty of perceived risk. Most children and many adults love the idea of swinging on a rope. Those who are not very confident can be encouraged to take this risk, with plenty of help if needed. Teamwork is important in this exercise. If some people take the risk and slip off the rope, they will hopefully get little more than muddy or wet. But as a result of trying, they may be more willing to pursue risks in future.

Tightrope walking

Materials needed

A length of strong rope.

Instructions

This exercise involves a client balancing on a rope and walking a short distance along it, with support if needed from a person each side.

This is an extremely difficult exercise and is best done in stages. You might start by stretching out the rope on the ground and getting people to balance as they walk along it. If there is a fairly narrow fallen log available, get clients to balance and walk along this, with a person each side to offer support if needed. Once people are confident in these initial activities they can progress to the suspended rope.

Tie the rope between two stout trees, about 60 cm (2 feet) from the ground. Ensure that the rope is level and as tight as possible (some ropes are more stretchy than others) and that the knots you use are secure enough to support the weight of the heaviest participant. It is best to clear the ground of any hazardous branches and rocks in case of injuries as the result of a fall.

Divide the group into teams of three. Each person has a turn walking along the rope, with available support from a person each side of the rope. The walk is probably best done with shoes off so that the client gets some grip with his/her feet. The two assistants help the participant to get on the rope. The best way to do this is for them to stand straight and solid each side of the rope and for the middle person to use their shoulders to support his/her weight. Once the client is on the rope and balanced, the two assistants hold their hands up flat while the tightrope walker touches their hands with his/her own hands to give a little balance and security. Only if the participant loses balance is it necessary to grab or hold hands or arms.

When people are completely confident with this exercise you can move on to the next stage. Again, tie the rope level between two trees. This time find an area where the ground gently slopes downwards. This will mean that the rope is 60 cm (2 feet) off the ground at one end and possibly 120 cm (4 feet) off the ground at the other.

Warning: The biggest danger in this exercise is falling with one leg each side of the rope. It is best to warn clients about this danger and to say that if they start to fall, they need to lean towards one side of other of the rope.

Objectives

Tightrope Walking is not an activity for the fainthearted. Nevertheless, when clients succeed in such a difficult task they will have every reason to celebrate. It is good for building confidence and for giving the nonverbal message to people that if they can succeed in this, any emotional problem – however big – can be conquered. The team effort needed and the gentle physical contact involved will hopefully make this a memorable and confidence-building exercise.

Mexican wave

Materials needed

None.

Instructions

This is a group activity that is both scary and lots of fun. Get the group to form two lines, facing each other, to create a long corridor. The participants put their arms out straight so that each person's arms overlap those of the person opposite by about a hand's length.

Clients take it in turns to walk through the corridor of arms. As the person reaches a pair of arms they lift them up to let him/her pass, then quickly come down again. The result is a Mexican wave effect of rising and falling arms as the person walks through.

The person joins in making the corridor at the top end of the line and the next person starts from the other end.

After everyone has had a turn and is confident, try speeding up the process. Get people to walk faster, then run and finally run at full speed. Of course, this needs the full cooperation of every team member to avoid injury.

If people are successful so far, why not finish with getting everyone moving their arms up and down rapidly together, only stopping to allow the person to pass through? When this is done successfully, it will definitely have been worth taking the extra risk.

Objectives

The Mexican Wave enables clients to take a risk with a group of people they know. It helps in team-building and cooperation and is a fairly safe way to explore the need many people have to take risks. After you have finished the activity, consider asking clients what the activity was like for them.

Achievements

In life you should not pursue goals that are easily achieved. Develop an instinct for what can be only just achieved through your greatest efforts.
– Unknown

No one ever achieved greatness by playing it safe.
– Harry Gray

Nothing splendid has ever been achieved except by those who dared believe that something inside of them was superior to circumstance.
– Bruce Barton

Introduction

Although achievement is not essential for self-esteem it is a requirement for character building. Through physically, mentally and emotionally challenging activities in the outdoors clients develop character, also known as 'mental toughness'. Ellis Cashmore writes: 'Character can be reduced to four constituents: (1) the capacity to overcome adversity and ultimately triumph; (2) the competence to lead others; (3) the ability to resist the temptation to transgress, ie break rules; and (4) altruism, the regard for others' interests and welfare above one's own' (Cashmore, 2002, page 50).

The individual and group activities in this section are designed to stretch people's abilities. They will be sharpened physically through exertion, the use of their muscles and the flow of adrenaline. Their mental abilities will be stretched as they work out situations and problems that need overcoming. They will be challenged emotionally as they face their fears – and do it anyway.

If clients become discouraged, get them to try again. Offer some help only if necessary and then only if they want it.

Encourage them to keep trying until they achieve their goal. Then celebrate their success with them.

Aiming straight

Materials needed

None.

Instructions

Aiming Straight involves participants moving in a straight line across a field or open area of the forest, avoiding bumping into other people or tripping over obstacles.

Invite people to find a place where they can stand by themselves. Then get them to concentrate on a spot somewhere on the other side of the field. At a given signal (say, when a whistle is blown) they are to move to that point in a straight line, staying fully focused on it but avoiding crashing into people or tripping over obstacles on the way.

After they have done this two or three times, get them to pick up speed, walking at a fast pace and then running towards the point. For a bit of variety, get them to focus on the point, then move to it backwards. Then try the same thing, first with very short steps (as many as possible), then with very long leaps to reduce the number of steps involved.

If you are working with a team, get them to pair up and move together across the field to the spot they have chosen. They can do this holding hands, linking arms back-to-back or supporting each other as they each hop on one leg. Depending on the ability of the participants, consider piggyback carrying, wheelbarrows or wheels (each person holding the ankles of his/her partner and rolling over and over like a wheel). There may be other ways of Aiming Straight that you or the participants can think of. Keep trying new ways until everyone is exhausted or until time runs out.

Objectives

This is an exercise involving movement, focusing and awareness. It requires a lot of concentration in order to be successful. Working as a group promotes the building of relationships and provides appropriate and safe physical contact.

Grasshoppers

Materials needed

None.

Instructions

When a grasshopper jumps, it uses the extra force of it longest pair of legs to propel itself high into the air. This is an exercise in imitating that jump. Instead of having extra-long legs, the client has a person on each side of him/her to give that extra boost.

After they are warmed up and ready for physical activity, get people into groups of three. The three then hold hands. The middle person of each group is the one who is going to jump, starting from a crouched position. The task of the two people holding hands each side is to assist the middle one to jump higher and higher with each successive jump.

Invite the clients to keep going until the person feels ready to stop, then swap around. Remind them that the person in the middle may suddenly feel a bit anxious and suggest they watch for this and stop immediately it happens.

Be aware that if the timing is not just right, the middle person's arms could be wrenched up with some force. As the facilitator, make sure you step in quickly if you see anyone deliberately pulling arms at the wrong time.

Objectives

Done properly, Grasshoppers will give clients a feeling of elation as they almost fly up into the air. Even a person who has not accomplished much in sport can achieve good results with this activity. It can help in boosting confidence and enabling clients to learn cooperation and care for each other.

Landmines

Materials needed

Natural objects such as small rocks or logs, to serve as landmines. Blindfolds.

Instructions

In this exercise participants cross a 'minefield' blindfolded without detonating any of the landmines. Choose an area such as an open field in which to place the landmines. If you are working in a forest, instead of using separate objects, you might say that every tree, however small, is a potential mine that will blow up if anyone touches it.

Explain to the clients that this is a serious exercise and needs lots of trust and concentration. Participants then pair up. One person in each pair is blindfolded and not allowed to talk. The person's partner can see and talk but is not allowed to enter the minefield or touch the other person. The blindfolded partner walks from one side of the minefield to the other by listening to the instructions of her/his partner. Give the pairs three minutes to work out their communication instructions. If you are working with young children, you might need to help them with deciding clear commands for stop, go, left and right. Then all the blindfolded people begin crossing the minefield *together.*

If anyone touches a landmine, he/she stands still for one minute before continuing. Once everyone has finished, the partners swap the blindfolds and are given another three minutes to plan their communication system before starting.

While the activity is taking place, you as the facilitator need to move around the area to make sure everyone is safe and that blindfolded people don't bump into each other. It is important that everyone succeeds to get across the area, however slowly.

After the exercise is finished, you may want to discuss with the clients how they experienced it. Did they trust their partner at the beginning? If so, what score out of 10 would they give their partner? What was their trust like at the end? What is important for trusting someone else in this way? What did their partner say or do to help them feel safe and secure? What were the best ways to communicate?

Objectives

Minefield is an exercise in communication, relationship building and trust. It needs courage and determination. Clients can only achieve success if they listen to each other. For people who have been let down by others in the past, the element of trust placed in another person is a major step towards their inner healing.

Emergency!

Materials needed

Two long and strong wooden poles, an old coat and a length of rope. Ketchup or similar substance for pretend blood.

Instructions

This activity needs the cooperation of an adult or teenager who may not be known to the participants. The idea is that the clients go on, say, a walk and suddenly find someone who appears injured but conscious. If the person found uses obviously false blood such as ketchup, the experience may not be quite as scary as it would be with stage blood. For adults and older young people you might like to extend the injuries to include a possible broken leg or arm that needs splinting and bandaging.

Once the person has been found, you as the facilitator tell the clients that this is an 'emergency' and they have to carry the person to a safe place without making his/her injuries worse. The distance can be anything from 50 to 400 metres, depending on the physical ability of the group. Point out that nearby there just happens to be two long poles, an old coat and some rope. (Also mention, if appropriate, that there are old bandages and short straight branches to serve as splints.) No further instructions are needed at this stage.

People will probably get into a discussion about ways to move the person. The discussion may result in the participants deciding simply to pick up the person together, without any of the props. If they start actually doing this they must be stopped. Picking up someone unconscious in this way from the ground could injure people's backs. If it was a real-life situation it could also seriously injure the person who had been found.

The ideal is that the group make a stretcher using a rope between the two poles. The rope stretched back and forth between the two parallel poles becomes the bed of the stretcher. Then the old coat is placed on top of the rope to make the stretcher comfortable. The stretcher is placed next to the injured person, who is carefully rolled on to it. Anything near to this ideal is acceptable. But as the facilitator it is your responsibility to ensure that the stretcher they make will hold the weight of the volunteer. This can be done by ensuring that each end of the loose rope is tied securely to one of the two poles.

Once the injured person is on the stretcher the group carefully lift it up and begin the carrying process. Again, as the facilitator, you need to ensure absolute safety in the lifting and carrying. Make sure people bend their knees, keeping their backs straight, and then all lift together. This will not be a problem, even for young children, if there are enough of them and it they lift correctly. You or one of the participants could walk in front to make sure there are no rocks or tree stumps that could result in someone tripping. Putting the stretcher down at the place of safety is a reversal of the process. Together they lower the stretcher, keeping their backs straight.

If people are confused about what to do at any stage, it is fine to give them hints and ideas. However, it is better not to tell them exactly what to do because that hinders them taking the initiative.

It might be useful afterwards to discuss what the experience was like for each of those taking part. What roles did they take? What initiative did they use? You might also invite the volunteer to say what the experience was like for him or her. How safe did he/she feel? Any positive comments about the participants' performance would be useful.

Objectives

Emergency! will almost certainly be a major challenge to most groups. The main objective, apart from how to handle a real emergency, is to help clients achieve success through team cooperation. Be aware of how the group members interact – the ones who always volunteer and those who are passive; those who come up with creative solutions and those who always rely on others.

Hand and feet sculptures

Materials needed

None.

Instructions

This is a team exercise in which people cooperate to make 'sculptures' using just their hands or feet. If you are working with a large group, you might get them to divide into smaller teams. Choose a dry grassy place because this exercise involves sitting or even lying down to get the best results.

Hand sculptures are made by ensuring that everyone's hands touch together to produce a sculpture that you as the facilitator ask for. Once the group has been successful (after you have all celebrated the result and possibly taken a photograph) they move on to the next sculpture, and so on. Ideas for the various sculptures could be a human face, bird, butterfly, dolphin and deer. Getting the hands in the right position will require quite a lot of discussion and also manoeuvring of bodies (standing, sitting, lying down). Otherwise, some people will be standing in front of the sculpture that is being created.

Feet sculptures are best done barefoot if participants can overcome their worry about having smelly feet! A less satisfactory alternative is everyone keeping their socks on. Start by getting everyone to sit in a circle, feet in front of them. They move their feet apart until they touch the foot of their neighbour on each side. Then they all lie back, lifting their feet in the air, each foot touching someone else's foot. The result hopefully will be a circle of cogs, each cog consisting of two feet held together high in the air. Then suggest they move closer into the centre to produce a perfectly joined-up circle with their feet.

After getting used to manoeuvring their feet to form cogs and a circle, the group will probably be ready to try some other foot sculptures. These could include a crocodile, boat, car, tall building and big wheel (or Ferris wheel). Again, call out the sculptures one at a time and pause between each for a photograph and/or a verbal celebration of success in this tricky activity.

Objectives

Hand and Feet Sculptures is an activity in team cooperation in which every team member plays a vital part. Clients with low confidence will be thrilled to achieve reasonable results. The activity also involves gentle physical contact, and this may be a help to people who have been abused or in other ways traumatised and who have difficulty with physical contact. People on the autistic spectrum may find the physical contact difficult but may forget this in their enthusiasm to achieve a good sculpture. In both cases, however, be prepared if the person decides not to take part.

Mud climb

Materials needed

Old clothes and trainers/walking boots. Hiking sticks (homemade or shop bought).

Instructions

Find in advance a steep slope reasonably free of vegetation. The ideal place is where a small river or stream cuts through a wooded area. The shading from the trees often keeps the slopes on both sides free of vegetation and reasonably damp. The mud might not be obvious until it is tested.

The idea is to clamber up one of the slopes, getting to the top as quickly as possible. This sounds relatively easy. The trouble is, the underlying mud causes feet to slip. As the slope becomes steeper towards the top, the task becomes even more difficult. There will almost certainly be plenty of slips, with people getting dirty or possibly even covered in mud.

To assist in the task participants will probably want to use a stick as well as holding on to tree trunks, branches and roots to help get to the top.

This can be an extremely difficult exercise that will result in clients being worn out. Be aware of smaller children and those not used to physical exertion. Instead of these people giving up, encourage older or stronger group members to extend a stick from above to assist the person to go up through a difficult part. Then the person can celebrate his/her success with the rest of the group.

Objectives

Clients who succeed with Mud Climb deserve to celebrate this as a major achievement. To get to the top they will probably have overcome their initial fear as their feet start sliding. They will have learned ways to stop themselves from going down instead of up. They will have overcome tired legs that want to give up. It is important for the facilitator and the other team members to praise their efforts and to point out what a lot of difficulties they had to deal with in order to reach the top.

Sneakers

Materials needed

'Camouflage' clothes for the participants (using natural colours such as greens, yellows and browns, or camouflage trousers). Hats in neutral colours. Camouflage face paints or natural paints made from mud and crushed leaves.

Instructions

Sneakers is an exercise in which camouflaged participants attempt to get from one place to another, past one or more observers, without being seen.

Find an area of the outdoors where there are plenty of hiding places. This could be an area of woodland or a place in the open where there are large rocks. Then help the clients to get into camouflage gear. Listen to their ideas, not just give your own. Hands and faces are best blended into the background. Use paint or mud/plant juices on hands and (with care) on faces. (Avoid contact with the eyes, because these materials could sting or even injure delicate eyes.) People can then find small plants, branches, grasses, or whatever they decide, to put over their faces, held in place with their hats.

Once everyone is in full camouflage, the idea is that they cross from one area to another without being seen by you and any other helpers with you. If you are working with a large group, divide them into two and get the groups to start from opposite sides, crossing over in the middle and heading for the place where the other side started. Perhaps they could have a competition to see which group completes the task first. This means that every team member, even the least able, reaches the other side.

Clients might crawl along the ground or quickly run from one tree/rock to another. If a person is running in the open and you can clearly see him/her, you might consider saying something like: 'I can see you. How about if you get down really low? Then it'll be difficult for me to see you.'

Be sure to give plenty of encouragement for achievement in this difficult but incredibly fun activity.

Warning: The main hazard for participants is that of adders if they are crawling around rocks on a warm, sunny day. Warn people to look before putting their hands on a rock and not pick up any interesting looking animal, thinking it is a frog or a lizard. It is very unlikely that an adder will attack unless provoked.

Objectives

Sneakers enables clients to achieve and enjoy their success. It is a good exercise for those who have low confidence and self-esteem. Perfectionists such as those on the autistic spectrum will hopefully excel at this activity. It is also good for teamwork and teambuilding as people help each other to look inconspicuous.

'My achievements'

Materials needed

Large pieces of coloured card cut into the shape of shields. Coloured felt-tips, pencils, pens, glue. Dried natural objects.

Instructions

Ideally, this exercise is the last in a series, weekend or week of therapeutic adventure activities. Invite the clients to make a banner celebrating all their achievements in the activities they have done.

Explain that in some countries, including the UK, important people such as kings, princes and lords traditionally designed a family Coat of Arms in the shape of a shield divided into four sections. This would be placed on sides of buildings with pictures to show various achievements within the family – usually those of the head of the family. If possible, find a Coat of Arms on the internet and print it out to show an example.

This exercise involves each client making his or her own Coat of Arms. They can use drawings and natural objects glued on to the shield to illustrate their personal achievements. Examples could include what they have learned, what they have discovered about themselves, how they have changed and how those changes are going to affect them in the future.

Once they have finished their Coats of Arms, invite people to talk about their achievements (if they want to) and make sure that they are applauded and praised for their personal successes.

Objectives

'My achievements' enables clients to consolidate their therapeutic and emotional learning. It provides a forum for them to show their successes to others in a way that is safe for them.

Relaxation and enjoyment

Introduction

How do relaxation and enjoyment fit in with therapeutic adventure? Surely they are a contradiction in terms?

It is an established medical fact that being relaxed reduces the level of negative emotions, especially anxiety, anger and scare. The person's breathing slows down, the muscles relax and the body temperature is reduced. Learning to relax is important for many athletes, who use relaxation techniques just before entering competition. It is also vital for other people who may or may not have emotional difficulties.

Most of us enjoy seeing dolphins. These beautiful creatures have much to teach us about relaxation and enjoyment. The people who are like dolphins 'weave their way through the storms of life, swimming through the eddying currents, knowing how to turn stress to their advantage. Dolphins see stress in a positive light, as an obstacle to overcome and learn from. Dolphins have a high level of self-esteem. They are satisfied with themselves, and with life in general' (Smith & Day, 1995, page 35).

A report by the UK charity Mind (2007) suggests that a relaxing walk in an area of nature can reduce depression. Almost all of those who participated reported that such 'green activities' had benefited their mental health, lifting depression. What people found relaxing were natural and social connections, sensory stimulation, outdoor activity and escape from the pressures and stresses of modern life.

Creative visualisation and labyrinth walking can also assist with emotional difficulties. 'When you learn to use creative visualisation constructively, you will spend short, regular periods of meditation, imagining yourself as calm and relaxed in these formerly threatening situations. You will start to see yourself as a more easy-going, self-confident person. In this way, you will gradually replace the negative image with a positive one' (US Gyms, 2008).

Oak tree's special gift

Materials needed

None.

Instructions

Oak Tree's Special Gift is a creative visualisation that works best outdoors. Find a large tree, preferably an oak tree, to sit under. You might consider getting the group to sit on the roots, with their backs to the trunk. Explain that you are going to tell a story and invite the clients to close their eyes if they want to and use their imaginations as you tell it. The suggested wording is as follows:

Imagine you are walking through the forest. (PAUSE.) While you walk along you see lots of tall, majestic trees. (PAUSE.) In the distance you notice a much bigger tree. (PAUSE.) It has spreading branches full of lovely, green leaves. (PAUSE.)

As you get nearer to the tree you see its huge strong trunk, rising up from the forest floor higher and higher. The trunk is so huge that it would need lots of people holding hands to form a circle around it. (PAUSE.)

You start to walk around the tree, looking at the trunk, then up at the branches and leaves. (PAUSE.) As you walk around, you notice a place where there is a small hole near the bottom of the trunk. (PAUSE.) It's surrounded by bark that has bulged out to form an arch, a bit like half a rubber tyre. (PAUSE.)

You walk towards the hole, trying to look inside. (PAUSE.) Then you notice that with a bit of effort you could squeeze your whole body through the hole. (PAUSE.) You hesitate for a moment, not sure what to do. (PAUSE.) Be aware of how you feel about going through the hole. (PAUSE.) Then you decide to go through the hole and into the tree itself.

(PAUSE.) Once inside, you stay still for a few moments until your eyes adjust to the darkness. (PAUSE.)

It's then that you start to notice a set of stairs going down right into the heart of the oak. (PAUSE.) You pause for a moment, wondering what to do. (PAUSE.) Be aware of how you feel about going down the stairs. (PAUSE.) You decide to take the risk. (PAUSE.) You walk carefully down, one step at a time. (PAUSE.)

At the bottom of the stairs, you see a door. (PAUSE.) You wonder what's on the other side of the door. (PAUSE.) Be aware of how you feel about opening the door. (PAUSE.) You push the door open and walk into the room. (PAUSE.) The room doesn't have any windows but by now you can see clearly. (PAUSE.)

That's when you notice the beautiful wooden box in the middle of the room. (PAUSE.) It is a large box that comes up to your knees and is a bit wider than your arms stretched right out. (PAUSE.) The box is made of oak, with beautiful carvings all over it. (PAUSE.) You notice the lid. (PAUSE.) You wonder what it would be like to open the lid and see what's inside. (PAUSE.) Be aware of how you feel about looking in the box. (PAUSE.) You decide to lift the lid and see what's inside. (PAUSE.)

There in the box is something special, a gift that you've always known you needed. (PAUSE.) It's something special that will help you solve your problems. Look at the gift's size, its colour and its texture. (PAUSE.) It can be yours simply by picking it up. (PAUSE.) Be aware of how you feel about picking up the special gift. (PAUSE.) Now, when you're ready, pick the gift up in your imagination. (PAUSE.) Look at it, feel it, enjoy it. (PAUSE.)

If you want, bring the oak tree's special gift very close towards your heart and then let it become a part of you. (PAUSE.) Be aware of how you are feeling now that you are using the special gift to help solve your problems. (PAUSE.)

OK, we've now finished the visualisation. When you're ready, open your eyes and come back into the here and now in this forest sitting against this tree.

Once people have finished the visualisation some of them might be willing to say what it was like for them. Be ready for others to remain silent, possibly because the result was so powerful for them.

Objectives

This visualisation is about reaching out for a source of strength that can help clients solve their own problems. It centres around an oak tree. The oak is solid, and has stood the test of time, often for hundreds of years. A gift that can change a client's life needs to come from a trustworthy and reliable source.

It is not necessary for the therapist to know what the problem is that needs solving. The visualisation will enable people to take the gift they need in order to release themselves from the problem.

Please note that, as in other visualisations, clients on the autistic spectrum, including those with Asperger's, may struggle with metaphors and instead take things literally.

My special house

Materials needed

Pencils, felt-tip pens and paper for each participant.

Instructions

Get the clients to find somewhere comfortable to sit down, perhaps on the grass, on logs or on rocks. Invite them to close their eyes and use their imaginations. Then begin this creative visualisation, speaking slowly, with plenty of time between phrases:

> Here in nature you are completely away from houses. So this is about a house in your imagination.
> You are walking along the mountain path. (PAUSE.) As you walk you see a house. (PAUSE.) Look at it. (PAUSE.) Notice its details. (PAUSE.) Walk towards it. (PAUSE.) What do you notice about it? (PAUSE.) You start to walk all around the house, looking at it as you walk. (PAUSE.)
> Now, you're halfway round. (PAUSE.) Notice the details of the house as you continue to walk around it. (PAUSE.) You have come back to where you were when you started. (PAUSE.)
> As you walked around the house you noticed a way to get in. (PAUSE.) Now go into the house. (PAUSE.) What do you see? (PAUSE.) Explore the house. (PAUSE.) What's inside? (PAUSE.)
> As you are exploring you notice a secret door leading to a secret room. (PAUSE.) Go inside that room. (PAUSE.) What do you see? (PAUSE.) Now leave the secret room and go back into the main part of the house. (PAUSE.)
> Now you are leaving the house. (PAUSE.) As you are walking away from it, you look back at it one more time. (PAUSE.) You are back on the mountain path once again, walking. (PAUSE.)

Now, write down or draw the house you saw in your imagination.

When everyone has finished their drawing, discuss what the exercise was like for the children.

Objectives

My Special House is a creative visualisation that can be used with clients to help them explore their own view of themselves and the protective system around them. People can notice for themselves any shortfalls in their drawings and decide to make appropriate changes in their lives.

This exercise can also be used as a therapeutic assessment. After you have collected the drawings look at the size and shape of the house. How big is the door in proportion to the rest of the house? Does it have a handle? (The shape depends on the person's cultural background.) How big or small are the windows? Does the house have a chimney? Is there smoke coming out of the chimney? (This is an indication of life and is present even in cultures where houses are not built with chimneys.) What is the setting (if any) around the house like? Is it a pleasant area to live?

Note any deficits in each client's house and consider what therapeutic interventions may be needed to help the person.

On your own in nature

Materials needed

Notebooks or pieces of paper and pens/pencils.

Instructions

Being on your own in nature is something that everyone can find helpful. Clients who have never done it before may find it a very powerful exercise.

As the facilitator, find in advance an area of nature where people can spread out but still be seen by you. An example might be a sloping hill where you stand at the bottom and the clients spread out away from each other but always in sight of you. Light woodland is ideal because there are places for each person to be alone. Make sure there is shelter from the sun if you are doing this exercise in high summer or in a country with very hot sun.

Explain to the clients that they are each going to spend some time alone in nature. Most adults may manage for an hour. If you are working with young children it may be best to plan on just 30 or 40 minutes, perhaps even less. Here is some suggested wording:

Find a place where you can be alone in nature. Keep within this area. [Explain the limits of the area you have chosen]. *Then, when I blow the whistle, stay silently and begin your time alone. You might want to sit or lie on the ground, sit on a rock or log or even climb up in a tree.*

During your time alone you might want to write or draw. There are pens and some paper here. You might just want to think or meditate. You may want to pray. Whatever you decide, make it a very special time just for you.

Five minutes before the end of our time alone I'll blow the whistle. When you hear this second whistle please finish your time alone and start gathering back here. We'll then talk together about the experience.

In the feedback, ask what the experience was like for the clients. Sitting in silence may be a completely new thing for some of them. Some might have found it very effective. Others might have been bored. There may be some negative comments as well as positive ones, and this is perfectly acceptable. Some of the experiences may be very personal to the clients and it is important to respect their privacy by not obliging them to speak. Others may be happy to show any drawings or written material.

Objectives

Scott Peck (1987/1988) writes: 'More than half of Beethoven's music is silence. Without the silence there is no music; there is only noise.' This exercise is designed to help people make the most of silence in life and in nature. In one sense silence in life is just as important as activity. Clients can become calm for a few minutes and have a chance to think and just be.

It is difficult to be prescriptive about the objectives of this exercise because it means something different to every individual. Objectives might range from calming down from the pressures of life to giving time to make new decisions. Be ready for some surprising effects in people as a result of being on their own in nature.

The labyrinth journey

Materials needed

Natural markers such as stones, pieces of wood or bark. Some wool or string to make the labyrinth boundaries clearer. A selection of play therapy objects such as cars, people, animals and precious things (gems, heroes, angels, religious symbols, etc).

Instructions

The Labyrinth Journey involves making a special course on the forest floor, in a field or other open space. The participants then together or individually go on a creative journey into the centre of the labyrinth and out again.

Labyrinths have been around for thousands of years. In English, the word 'maze' refers to a labyrinth with false paths and dead ends. 'Labyrinth' refers to an open course that leads to the centre and then out again.

A labyrinth represents people's journey through time and experience. For hundreds of years the Christian church used labyrinths to represent the Christian on his spiritual journey. A famous religious labyrinth that still exists is at Chartres Cathedral, France, which was built in 1201. Today labyrinths are being introduced again in public open places, schools, hospitals, prisons and churches.

In therapeutic adventure and play therapy the labyrinth can be used in a nondirective way for clients who want to make an in-and-out type of journey in their therapy. It is ideal for an activity following a creative visualisation. It can also be used for endings, where people take in or out objects to represent some part of their life.

The labyrinth is ideal for many group activities. A bereavement group could use it to symbolise leaving the people they are grieving at the centre and moving out into the world again. We heard of one group making one on a beach at low tide, putting symbolic objects into the centre and journeying to the edge again. Then, while the tide washed away the labyrinth, they celebrated the lives of the people they had lost.

Explain to the participants that this exercise involves making a temporary labyrinth using stones and wool. Most labyrinths are right to left. For this activity we tend to use a simple right-to-left labyrinth. We have found that this can enhance creativity. The best way to start is to form the central cross shape with stones or pieces of bark and to work outwards from there. The wool is laid once the stones or pieces of wood are in place to ensure that people keep on the path. If you are working with young children, they may need considerable help to make a reasonable labyrinth.

The creative visualisation on the following page has been developed by Christine Day especially for use with a labyrinth of this type. Once people are relaxed and comfortable, with eyes closed if they want, tell the story.

A man was going on a long journey. He set off from home with his rucksack on his back and his hiking stick in his hand. *(PAUSE)*

He was whistling to himself as he set off in the sunshine and walked through the beautiful countryside. *(PAUSE)* Every few minutes he would stop to admire a flower or listen to a bird singing in a tree nearby. *(PAUSE)* Life was good, and the man was grateful for the fresh springs to drink from. He felt at one with nature. *(PAUSE)*

He travelled on and the path became steeper. As he walked, the man would collect interesting little stones, pinecones and other small treasures. *(PAUSE)* He would take photographs to add to his treasure of memories. *(PAUSE)*

The landscape was changing and becoming mountainous. The man had to go slower and sometimes stop to get his breath back. The journey wasn't so much fun now. *(PAUSE)* Sometimes he stumbled on loose rocks and scree. But still he struggled on. *(PAUSE)*

Occasionally he fell down. But the man wasn't going to give up. Who said it would be easy? *(PAUSE)* He knew that sometimes life wasn't fair. *(PAUSE)* He was sure that the journey would be worth it when he got there. *(PAUSE)*

When he reached the top of the mountain the man could hardly walk. Instead of admiring the beautiful view, he sat down and took his boots off. Then he began to count the blisters on his feet. *(PAUSE)*

After a while, the man stood up and tried to lift his rucksack. He couldn't move it. It was so heavy. *(PAUSE)* The man sat down again and unpacked his bag to find out why. *(PAUSE)*

He put everything on the ground around him and looked at it. He was shocked at what he found. Mixed in with his treasures were heavy rocks and useless boulders. *(PAUSE)* Every time he had found the journey difficult, or he had stumbled, he had put another rock or boulder in his bag. *(PAUSE)*

The man took out all the useless rocks and boulders that had accumulated. *(PAUSE)* He left them at the top of the mountain. *(PAUSE)* Then he carefully replaced his treasures. *(PAUSE)*

He lifted his rucksack easily and looked around him. The view was amazing. It took his breath away. *(PAUSE)* He could see all around him – valleys, streams, cattle eating the grass, a buzzard circling above him, a tiny village a long way below. *(PAUSE)* He imagined he could hear the shouts of children playing. In the distance there were more mountains. *(PAUSE)*

The man set off for home. Once again he enjoyed the journey. *(PAUSE)* He was determined not to pick up any more heavy rocks and useless boulders. From now on the man would be careful only to collect real treasure.

Now invite the clients, one after the other, to collect what they need and to go through the journey themselves. Passing each other in the labyrinth is part of the team exercise and enhances rather than detracts from the experience.

If for any reason it is not possible on the day to build a full size labyrinth, people can use their fingers to trace their journey on a photocopy of the labyrinth on an A4 sheet. Again, they can place objects where they want. Research has shown that miniature labyrinths such as these can also be effective with clients.

Objectives

The Labyrinth Journey is a creative visualisation that can be problem-solving in a relaxed and enjoyable way. People may want to go on the journey again and again. In this way they can deal with whatever is troubling them, leaving behind the 'rocks' that have hindered their journey and prevented them enjoying the beauty of life.

'I live in the leaves'

Materials needed

Clients will need spare, clean clothes after this exercise as they will almost certainly get both wet and dirty.

Instructions

This is an exercise in experiential creative visualisation that takes place in the leaves on the forest floor. It is important to find an area of the forest that is reasonably dry and relatively free of ants, which can sometimes bite.

Explain to the participants that they are going to lie in the leaves on the forest floor for a story. They need to know in advance that they will probably get a little wet and probably dirty, too, but that they can change into clean, dry clothes straight after the exercise. As they lie on the forest floor taking part in the visualisation, they will probably find that little creatures such as insects will crawl across them, even over their arms and faces. Explain that these creatures might tickle a bit but they will not harm them. *Warning: You as the facilitator will need to overcome any fears you might have in this area before you explain this to the clients. Otherwise they will pick up fear in your voice.*

Invite them to find a place to lie down, face up, with their eyes closed if they want. If they lie on anything prickly, they need to get up and remove it before the exercise begins. If they do not do this, they will find it difficult to concentrate.

Occasionally someone may find lying down too scary, so he/she might sit in the leaves instead. If you are working with a group, they could help put leaves carefully all over each other (even their faces) while they are lying down so that they feel even more involved.

Once everyone has settled, begin the visualisation, speaking slowly and with plenty of space for people to use their imaginations:

This is a story called 'I live in the leaves'. While I tell the story use your imagination without speaking or moving about.

I live in the leaves of the forest. (PAUSE.) I might be a little mouse or a shrew or a vole. (PAUSE.) I spend my life scrambling over the leaves and through them. (PAUSE.)

A lot of the time I'm looking for my food. (PAUSE.) I wonder what there is to eat today? (PAUSE.) Perhaps an insect or a caterpillar or a slug. (PAUSE.) Maybe there will be some berries or some nuts or some toadstools. (PAUSE.) Sometimes it's difficult to find enough food. (PAUSE.) Then I feel so, so hungry. (PAUSE.) Imagine what that's like for someone with a tiny body like mine. (PAUSE.) If I don't find food soon I'll die. (PAUSE.) But always, just when I think I might die, I find another good meal. (PAUSE.)

Sometimes it's cold and wet here. (PAUSE.) Imagine what that's like for little me. (PAUSE.) At other times the wind blows through the tops of the trees and makes a loud noise. (PAUSE.) The trees sound as if they're going to come crashing down on me. (PAUSE.) I'm little and helpless when the wind blows so strongly. (PAUSE.) Imagine what it's like for me then. (PAUSE.) But always I know the wind will pass and I'll feel safe again. (PAUSE.)

Sometimes I get really scared in the leaves. (PAUSE.) I hear these big birds making loud noises. (PAUSE.) I know they would eat me if they found me. (PAUSE.) At night the owls are the worst. (PAUSE.) They make such a huge noise it almost deafens me. (PAUSE.) Imagine what it's like for me when the owls make their noise. (PAUSE.) I'm glad I've got very good hearing and can quickly find a place to escape before those big birds catch me. (PAUSE.)

Each year I build a nest for my babies. (PAUSE.) They are so tiny and helpless. (PAUSE.) I want to make sure they are warm and safe. (PAUSE.) Sometimes other animals come looking for them. They are hungry and want to kill my babies. (PAUSE.) Imagine what that's like for me when I know they're around. (PAUSE.) But I know I've found a good place to put my nest. (PAUSE.) They're safe. I'm sure of that. (PAUSE.)

OK, when you're ready slowly open your eyes, sit up and come back to being here in the forest. Stand up, stretch, turn round once and come back to the present.

After finishing the visualisation, everyone goes back indoors to get changed. Then when they are clean and refreshed ask them what the visualisation was like for them. Avoid probing therapeutic-type questions. Just listen to what they have to say.

Objectives

The objective of the 'I live in the trees' visualisation is to enable clients to find within themselves the resources to get the emotional nourishment they need, to face their worst fears and to obtain self-protection. This visualisation is a powerful way for people to deal with their own problems and fears at an out-of-awareness level and in a fun and different way.

Tree impressions

Materials needed

Thin paper (such as photocopy paper), masking tape and thick crayons.

Instructions

Find a forest area with plenty of different kinds of trees, not just evergreens. Get the participants to look closely at the textures and patterns of bark on various trees. Then explain that together you are going to make impressions of tree bark using paper and crayons, similar to the way people make brass rubbings of plaques in churches and cemeteries.

Place a piece of paper against the dry bark. Although it is not entirely necessary, this can be held in place with long pieces of masking tape. (Cellophane tape can damage the bark.) Strip the paper (if any) off the crayons and use the side of them to rub gently across the piece of paper, taking an impression of the bark pattern underneath. This can take some practice to get right. It is best to do it in only one direction or the picture can become distorted. The temptation is to use the end of the crayon in the conventional way. This usually doesn't work well because there is a tendency to press too hard.

Once people have taken several tree impressions on different pieces of paper, look together at the impressions, noticing the various patterns and textures. Then, if it is appropriate, discuss with the clients the function and purpose of bark. Ask questions like:

Why do trees have bark? (Protection of the delicate internal structure of the tree, to prevent the vital sap inside from drying etc.)

Some trees shed the outer layers of bark. In what ways have people used these outer layers of bark? (Making corks, lining canoes, lighting fires using birch-bark as tinder, etc.)

What would happen if the tree didn't have its bark? (The tree would probably die.)

Objectives

This exercise is not only a fun way of discovering more about trees but a way for clients to consider their own system of emotional protection. As such it could be especially useful for those who have faced abuse or bullying or been in domestic violence situations.

As they explore the way that trees protect themselves using bark, clients will hopefully be considering at an out-of-awareness level how they defend themselves against bullying, abuse and emotional pressure. By discovering that trees must protect themselves for survival, people may make new decisions to strengthen their own protection system.

Looking at the way 'spare' bark can have important functions for people could at an unconscious level provide clients who have a strong protective system with the motivation to support those more vulnerable than themselves.

Leafy lines and patterns

Materials needed

Thin paper (such as photocopy paper), masking tape and a board for each participant. Pencils, felt-tip pens and thick crayons.

Instructions

Explain to the group that this exercise is about exploring the shapes and patterns of leaves. Get them to collect various kinds of leaves within the deciduous forest – dead leaves as well as ones growing on trees. The leaves don't all have to be perfect. Those of some trees are vulnerable to insect attack and damage. For instance, if there are some oak trees in the forest, search the living leaves for attractive red lumps that are the result of insects laying their eggs within the leaf structure.

Once people have collected enough leaves from different sources, look together at the various leaves, including the outline shapes, the lines (veins) on the back and any flaws that are present. Invite clients to trace around the leaves to get the outline shape, then draw in the veins and any other markings they see. If people have any leaves with raised veins, such as sycamore, they can make leaf rubbings instead. Put a leaf on the board so that the raised veins are uppermost. Place a piece of paper on top, possibly held in place with masking tape. Then gently rub the side of a crayon over the paper to produce the pattern.

Once all the pictures have been finished look together at them. Discuss interesting aspects of the leaves. Then, if it is appropriate, discuss the function and purpose of leaves. Ask questions like:

Why do trees have leaves? (To absorb sunlight and help the tree produce living material in order to grow; to provide the tree with lots of cells to breathe in carbon dioxide and breathe out oxygen.)

How do leaves make sure they get enough sunlight? (They continually move around to face the sun.)

Why do leaves turn red, brown and yellow in Autumn, then fall off the tree? (To remove impurities from the tree; to allow the tree to rest during the long winter; to make room for new growth in the Spring.)

What would it be like for us if trees never had leaves? (The forests would look very different in the summer; the air would be polluted because leaves remove a huge amount of the carbon emissions in the air.)

Objectives

Leafy Lines and Patterns is not just an outdoor education exercise. For many clients, in their out-of-awareness, leaves can parallel the positive aspects of their lives. Through having a good self-image they can draw positive comments from others ('strokes' or 'positive affirmations', which are the building blocks of life). In that sense, a healthy self-image turns us towards the light of helpful people around us and therefore get our needs met. A healthy self-image can be a first step in clients making new decisions about the way they respond in life, thus helping to remove the 'impurities' in their lives that have been the cause of many of their problems. It can even have a knock-on effect, influencing others around them towards a positive self-image.

Pictures from nature

Materials needed

Natural materials that people find in a forest. These can include:

dry leaves	bits of bark	feathers
seeds	acorn and nut shells	lichen

A camera to record the finished pictures.

Instructions

The therapist invites the participants to find a reasonably flat space on the forest floor where they will make their picture. They may want to clear away leaves and other debris. A clearing will have a thinner layer of leaves than a dense area of the forest. Some clients may want to put a miniature fence or boundary around their picture.

Once each area is ready, each person starts collecting objects for his or her picture, as above. Avoid living plants, and toadstools that may be poisonous or smell. Also, ensure that people do not pick any wild flowers. Either the therapist or the clients can suggest a theme for the pictures – my family, my favourite way to relax, the good things in my life, my problems all solved etc. Alternatively, the picture can be done in a nondirective way. In this case the clients collect the materials and make any picture they want that could help them solve their problems.

Once all the pictures are completed, you as the therapist may want to suggest that the group find ways of linking the pictures with each other. For instance, each person shows the rest of the group his/her picture and the group together see what links there are with the other pictures. Alternatively, twigs or branches could be used to link the pictures in a physical way.

Finally, invite people to spend a few moments (or minutes) looking at their creations in the context of the forest and just enjoying the sight, sound and smell.

Objectives

This activity is in some ways an extension of using natural objects in a sandtray. The added bonus is that clients have a whole forest in which to define their picture. Many people will enjoy finding their own natural materials and creating a picture in a woodland setting. The therapist will need to trust the process as she/he sees the pictures being created that can help solve the client's deepest problems, without always knowing what those problems might be.

Finding links between the pictures in a group context can help with group formation and functioning. It can also be a way to build confidence and self-esteem as people tell each other about their pictures and find that other people share the same joys and sorrows as they do.

Sources and references

Berne, Eric (1962). Classification of positions. *Transactional Analysis Bulletin, 1,* 3, page 23.

Berne, Eric (1973). *The structure and dynamics of groups and organisations*, New York: Ballantine. (Original work published 1963.)

Berne, Eric (1975). *What do you say after you say hello?* London: Corgi. (Original work published 1972.)

Berne, Eric (1994). *Principles of group treatment.* Menlo Park, California: Shea Books. (Original work published 1966.)

Boholst, FA (2002). A life position scale. *Transactional Analysis Journal 32,* 1, pages 28-32.

Boyslife (2008). World wide web: www.boyslife.org/outdoors

Brandes, Donna, & Phillips, Howard (1978). *Gamesters' Handbook: 140 games for teachers and group leaders.* London: Hutchinson. (Original work published 1977.)

Cashmore, Ellis (2002). *Sport Psychology: The key concepts.* London: Routledge.

Clark, Chris (2008). All Aboard leadership and groupwork training.
http://www.geocities.com/saskrescue/all_aboard/trust.htm

Dyer, Kirstia (2002). *Nature Awareness as a Therapy Modality.* World wide web:
http://journeyofhearts.org/resources/nature

Erikson, Erik (1968). *Identity, Youth and Crisis.* New York: Norton.

Gass, Michael, & Gillis, Lee (1995). CHANGES: An assessment model using adventure experiences. *The Journal of Experiential Education, 18,* 1, May 1995, pages 34-40.

Goodman, Robert (1999). *Strengths and Difficulties Questionnaire.* World Wide Web.

Griffiths, Ken (2002). *The Survival Manual.* London: Carlton Books.

Leben, Norma (1993-1999). *Directive Group Play Therapy: 60 structured games for the treatment of ADHD, low self-esteem and traumatised children.* Pflugerville, Texas: Morning Glory Treatment Center for Children.

Mabey, Richard (1972/2007). *Food for Free.* London: Collins.

Mind (2007). *Go green to beat the blues.* Mind week 12 to 19 May 2007. World wide web: www.mind.org.uk

Napper, Rosemary, & Newton, Trudi (2000). *Tactics: Transactional analysis concepts for all trainers, teachers and tutors, plus insight into collaborative learning strategies.* Ipswich: TA Resources.

Neill, James (2007). Adventure therapy and wilderness/nature therapy. www.wilderdom.com/adventuretherapy.html

Ray, Nick (2005). Transactions on the rock face. *Therapy Today,* December 2005, pages 15-17.

Richards, Kaye, & Peel, Jenny (2005). Outdoor cure. *Therapy Today,* December 2005, pages 4-8.

Schoel, J, Prouty, D, & Radcliffe, P (1988). *Islands of Healing: A guide to adventure based counselling.* Hamilton, Massachusetts: Project Adventure Inc.

Scott Peck, M (1988). *The Different Drum: Community making and peace.* New York: Touchstone. (Original work published 1987.)

Slesser, Malcolm (2004). *With Friends in High Places.* Edinburgh: Mainstream Publishing.

Smith, Robert, & Day, Roger (1995). Succeeding in a sea of stress. *Business Education Today,* September/October 1995, pages 35-37.

Tuckman, Bruce (1965). Developmental sequence in small groups. *Psychological Bulletin.*

US Gyms (2008). World wide web: www.usgyms.net/visualization.htm

USA Weekend (2005). Edition: 13 March 2005.

Wilderness Program (2008). World Wide Web: www.tas.gov.au

Wilson, Kate, & Ryan, Virginia (2005). *Play Therapy: A nondirective approach for children and adolescents,* Kate Wilson & Virginia Ryan, London: Baillière Tindall. (Original work published 1992.)

Appendix 1

Being OK, Keeping OK, by Roger Day

Being OK, Keeping OK
Roger Day

'You have to stay in shape. My grandmother, she started walking five miles a day when she was 60. She's 97 today and we don't know where the hell she is.'
Ellen DeGeneres, comedian, quoted in *Walker's Companion* (Ramblers' Association, 2004).

'The group therapist, like any physician, owes it to his patients to keep in good health . . . Regular outdoor exercise will give him more respect for the benefits of physical vitality and for the health of the body, which is the only known vessel for the human psyche. He should not allow the scepticism of his more self-indulgent or lazier colleagues to interfere with this old-fashioned and healthful régime.'
Eric Berne, psychotherapist, 'The First Three Minutes', *Principles of Group Treatment* (Berne, 1966/1994, 61-62).

In order for therapists to maintain their 'I'm OK, you're OK' position, they need to 'stay in shape' physically, emotionally, spiritually, recreationally and mentally. And what better way to do that than to escape from the busyness of everyday life by walking in the beautiful local countryside?

Countryside walking provides a wide range of experiences that are useful to the therapist. One of these is that walking in a particular locality helps the therapist in locating the self. Another is self-care. Therapists often encourage clients to care for themselves. It is a case of one finger pointed at others and three pointed at themselves. Here is an opportunity literally to 'walk the talk'. A third experience is the heightening of the five senses, or at least those senses that are actually available to the therapist. This heightening of the senses is sometimes called 'sensory acuity'.

Sensory acuity

In addition to *sight* (trees, flowers, hills) and *touch* (rough bark and weathered stones), the walker can *hear* the sounds of birds singing and brooks babbling. Then there are the *smells:* the fresh smells of grass and meadow flowers and the less salubrious smells of dank ravines and freshly dropped animal manure. There are even the *tastes* of hand-winnowed wheat, ripened berries and sweet pollen sucked from honeysuckle flowers.

Berne believed that a good clinician should use all five senses in diagnosis, assessment and treatment planning. While most therapists are skilled at sight and hearing, the other three senses are less well used. Berne writes: 'Good odours and bad odours should be noted, and this may require the resurrection of a sense of smell which has been severely repressed by social training . . . The sense of taste has become even more unfashionable as a clinical instrument than the sense of smell, even for diagnosing diabetes, and in group treatment there is seldom an occasion to use it unless the patient offers the therapist a candy, which may turn out to be sour or bitter' (Berne, !966/1994: 65).

While in other writings Berne saw very little use for touch in therapy, subsequent writers have stressed its importance as a therapeutic technique. Cornell writes: 'Through the continued use of touch, the therapist can more clearly communicate empathy and continued involvement while directly supporting increasing autonomy and activity. The therapist communicates and demonstrates at a body level that relatedness and closeness do not have to be sacrificed for competence and autonomy' (Cornell, 1997: 35).

Therapy doors

Walking in the countryside can help the therapist experiment around her own personality adaptations and therapy doors (see Ware, 1983).

If, for instance, she has a Conscientious Workaholic 'performing' personality adaptation, her contact door is Thinking, her target door is Feeling and her trap door is Behaviour. The trap door could rightly be renamed the 'closed door' because it is 'the area in which one will see the most significant changes as a result of therapy' (Joines & Stewart, 2002: 11). A trap door is usually in the floor and, when it is open, the unwary person may fall through it. A closed door, on the other hand, can be opened and walked through. Countryside walking can be seen as a way of opening that closed door.

After considering the options (Thinking) and getting enthusiastic about walking (Feeling), the therapist who goes on the walk (Behaviour) may be making contact with her inner self at a profound level. This could lead to new ways and patterns of behaving that could in turn lead to internal changes.

Multiple intelligences

Countryside walking can also be understood and appreciated in terms of different forms of intelligence. Dr Howard Gardner (1983, 2000) proposed eight different intelligences as an alternative to the traditional notion of intelligence based merely on IQ testing. These are:

* Linguistic intelligence ('word smart')
* Logical-mathematical intelligence ('number/reasoning smart')
* Spatial intelligence ('picture smart')
* Bodily-kinesthetic intelligence ('body smart')
* Musical intelligence ('music smart')
* Interpersonal intelligence ('people smart')
* Intrapersonal intelligence ('self smart')
* Naturalistic intelligence ('nature smart')

From Gardner's work Dr Thomas Armstrong (1994, 1998/2000) has developed eight different potential pathways to learning. He invites people, whatever they are teaching or learning, to connect with these pathways. The pathways are numbered below with indications of how they might relate to countryside walking.

1. Words (linguistic intelligence)

Get a good general book on walking and learn as much as possible about it. Read up on the planned walking route, including studying any walking guides available. Meet with others to discuss the route. Research any historical aspects of old railways or canals likely to be encountered. Write up the proposed route, highlighting anything from the research to look out for on the walk.

2. Numbers or logic (logical-mathematical intelligence)

Measure out the distance covered using a map measure, or with a pedometer while walking the actual route. Calculate the length of footstep and the number of steps.

Consider the wider implications of footsteps. Experts believe that although a person needs to walk 10,000 steps a day to be healthy, the average adult in the UK clocks up a mere 3000 steps.

The Walking the Way to Health Initiative (WHI) has distributed thousands of Step-O-Meters to members of the public who want to increase their amount of walking. These cost less than œ☐10 to buy. They can be lent free by doctors in geographical areas where there is a significant risk of heart disease. The 10,000-steps-a-day project was part of a five-year programme launched in October 2000 by the British Heart Foundation and the Countryside Agency.

Although more expensive, pedometers are excellent in checking the number of steps a person walks each day. They can also be calibrated to give mileage. The average adult needs to walk about four miles in order to achieve the target. A four-mile walk once a week is an added extra rather than a replacement for the 10,000 steps needed each day. Any shortfall in a particular day can be made up by walking instead of taking the car, using the stairs instead of taking the lift, dancing to music or running on the spot. The latter can add as much as 170 steps in just one minute if done at a fairly vigorous pace.

Looking at this approach logically in terms of the Ware sequence (Ware, 1983), Thinking (considering the number of steps and planning how to achieve them) is followed by Behaviour (clocking up the 10,000 steps) and then Feeling (exhilaration and joy at having succeeded). This does not fit in with the sequence of any of the six personality adaptations originally identified by Ware. Joines & Stewart (2002) ask the question: 'Are there only six personality adaptations? How would you know if you had found a seventh or eighth?' (22). Taking their point in a logical but lighthearted way, could Thinking (Contact Door), Behaviour (Target Door) and Feeling (Trap/Closed Door) be indications of a possible new personality adaptation?

3. Pictures (spatial intelligence)

Go to the local library and look at archived pictures of country areas, farms and buildings on the route. Study maps of the area, observing landmarks on the chosen paths. Imagine what things look like at different points, then check them out during the actual route. Take photographs or, even better, draw sketches of significant buildings and scenery during the walk. Look at these at the end of the walk and try to piece together visually the whole walk.

4. Music (musical intelligence)

The hills (and the valleys) really are alive with the sound of music! During a walk in the countryside listen to the sounds of the birds singing, water rushing down a stream, the rhythmic wind in the trees and even the swish of distant traffic on busy roads.

Singing or whistling in the countryside is an enjoyable pastime, and unlike the singer in the bath, there is no one around to complain! Think, too, of songs that focus on walking.

Consider that old-time favourite, 'I love to go a-wandering'. Or think of *The Snowman* film with 'Walking in the Air', the *Wizard of Oz* song 'Follow the Yellow Brick Road' or even the Goons' song 'I'm Walking Backwards to Christmas'! The possibilities are endless. Make a list of all the songs that focus on walking. It is a surprise to discover how many there are.

5. Self-reflection (intrapersonal intelligence)

There is nowhere better for self-reflection than in the heart of the countryside. Here, when on his own, a therapist can think about his direction in life, consider ways to take care of himself, explore his internal processes and analyse his motivations. Self-reflection can also encompass the spiritual dimension, whatever that means to the individual. This can include prayer, meditation or reflection on a higher being such as a Creator God or even Mother Nature.

6. A physical experience (body-kinesthetic intelligence)

Countryside walking by its nature is a very physical experience. Walking over rough terrain or newly ploughed fields, or traversing paths overgrown with brambles can be very physical indeed. Consider how much energy is consumed on a walk in terms of calories and how much fluid is lost through sweating. A vigorous walk in the countryside can be one of the most satisfying forms of exercise.

7. A social experience (interpersonal intelligence)

Talk with others about the planned route. Join a local ramblers' club and attend meetings. Walk with others and consider how walking can become a team effort as team members help each other over stiles and fences, through narrow gaps and up and down steep slopes. Consider the protective element as members of a group of walkers act as a protective barrier for those who are frightened of lively bullocks or curious horses.

8. An experience in the natural world (naturalistic intelligence)

There is no better way of experiencing the natural world than to walk in the midst of it. Regularly stop and observe nature. Look at insects rushing round on the woodland floor or a weasel rustling in the hedgerow as it stalks unsuspecting rabbits. Study various burrows and learn to detect from the size of the hole and any droppings around what animal has made them. Get to know plants that sting and those that heal, plants that are beautiful and those that are hideous. Find out the fungi that can be eaten and those equally beautiful that can kill. Chew the soft, succulent heart of certain grasses on a summer's day or taste the delicious berries in the autumn hedgerow. Breathe in the beauty of the natural world and, while you are in the countryside, let yourself become a part of it.

Summary

Therapists can keep in shape physically, emotionally, spiritually, recreationally and mentally by walking in the beautiful countryside. Walking can heighten the senses and enable the therapist to find new ways of thinking, feeling and behaving. By using the eight intelligences in creative ways the therapist can come to appreciate walking as a tool for taking care of herself and for expanding her 'toolkit' of ways of helping her clients.

References

Armstrong, Thomas (1994). *Multiple Intelligences in the Classroom.* Alexandria, VA: Association for Supervision and Curriculum Development.

Armstrong, Thomas (1998/2000). *Multiple intelligences.* Armstrong's website on the worldwide web:
www.thomasarmstrong.com/multiple_intelligences.htm

Berne, Eric (1994). *Principles of Group Treatment.* Menlo Park, California: Shea Books. Original work published 1966.

Cornell, Bill (1997). Touch and boundaries in TA: Ethical and transferential considerations. *Transactional Analysis Journal,* 27 (1), 30-37.

Gardner, Howard (1983). *Frames of Mind: The theory of multiple intelligences.* New York: Basic.

Gardner, Howard (1983). *Multiple Intelligences: The theory in practice.* New York: Basic.

Gardner, Howard (2000). *Intelligence Reframed: Multiple intelligences for the 21st century.* New York: Basic.

Joines, Vann, & Stewart, Ian (2002). *Personality Adaptations.* Nottingham: Lifespace Publishing.

Ramblers' Association (2004). *The Walker's Companion.* London: The Ramblers' Association.

Ware, Paul (1983). Personality adaptations (doors to therapy). *Transactional Analysis Journal,* 13 (1), 11-19.

Printed in Great Britain
by Amazon